Table of Contents

Introduction 6
The Evolution of Hoop Dreams on the Big Screen 6
Selecting Cinema's 10 Most Pivotal Productions 9
Mapping the Game Plan: An Inside Look at the Films Chosen
.... 12
Chapter 1 - Space Jam (1996) 15
Spinning a Hollywood Fantasy Starring Michael Jordan 15
Blending Live-Action with Beloved Looney Tunes Characters
.... 19
Commercial Success and Enduring Pop Culture Impact 24
The Peak of Jordan's Global Stardom and Brand Power 28
Chapter 2 - Hoosiers (1986) 33
Bringing the True Story of the Milan Miracle to Screen 33
Gene Hackman Anchors the Underdog Sports Drama 38
Capturing the Magic of Indiana High School Hoops 43
Cementing Its Place as a Sports Movie Classic 48
Chapter 3 - Love & Basketball (2000) 53
Gina Prince-Bythewood Puts a Fresh Spin on NBA Dreams ..53
Omar Epps and Sanaa Lathan's Chemistry Powers the
Narrative 59
A Nuanced Perspective on Young Black Love and Aspirations
.... 65
The Rare Basketball Movie Led by a Woman's Perspective 71
Chapter 4 - He Got Game (1998) 77
Spike Lee's Stylistic Take on Basketball Dreams 77
Denzel Washington as a Convict Father, Ray Allen as a
Phenom Son 83
Examining the Ethics of NCAA Recruiting and Scouting 88

Lee's Signature Flair in Service of a Basketball Story 93
Chapter 5 - White Men Can't Jump (1992)................**100**
An Irreverent Buddy Comedy Set in LA Pickup Games 100
Wesley Snipes and Woody Harrelson's Unlikely Bond 108
Exploring Racial and Class Stereotypes with Humor 115
Cult Following for Snipes and Harrelson's Chemistry..........122
Chapter 6 - Coach Carter (2005) **128**
Bringing the Story of Ken Carter's Crusade to Screen 128
Samuel L. Jackson Leads with Gravitas and Inspiration 135
Emphasizing Education Alongside Athletic Dreams.............142
Wrestling With Sports Movie Tropes and Clichés 150
Chapter 7 - Eddie (1996).. **157**
Fictional Comedy Starring Whoopi Goldberg as a Coach 157
Fish Out of Water Tale of a NYC Fan Turned Coach.............163
Another Underdog Team Overcoming Odds 171
One of Several '90s Films Focused on Coaches...................... 177
Chapter 8 - Glory Road (2006)............................... **182**
Chronicling Texas Western's Barrier-Breaking Title............182
Josh Lucas as Pioneering Coach Don Haskins 188
*Examining the Racial Tensions of College Hoops in the '60s*194
*Taking Some Dramatic License With Events and Timelines*200
Chapter 9 - Blue Chips (1994) **206**
Nick Nolte as a College Coach Compromised Morally 206
Exposing Recruiting Corruption and Ethical Quandaries....212
Cast of NBA Stars and College Talent.................................. 217
More Cynical Take on NCAA Machinations 222
Chapter 10 - Hoop Dreams (1994)...........................**228**
Steve James' Landmark Documentary Following Two Preps *228*

Copyright © 2023 by Sophia M. Johnson (Author)

All rights reserved. This book or any portion thereof may not be reproduced or used in any manner whatsoever without the express written permission of the publisher except for the use of brief quotations in a book review.

This book is copyright protected. This is only for personal use. You cannot amend, distributor, sell, use, quote or paraphrase any part or the content within this book without the consent of the author.

Please note the information contained within this document is for educational and entertainment purposes only. Every attempt has been made to provide accurate, up to date and reliable complete information. No warranties of any kind are expressed or implied. Readers acknowledge that the author is not engaging in the rendering of legal, financial, medical or professional advice. The content of this book has been derived from various sources. Please consult a licensed professional before attempting any techniques outlined in this book.

By reading this document, the readers agree that under no circumstances are the author responsible for any losses, direct or indirect, which are incurred as a result of the use of information contained within this document, including but not limited to errors, omissions or inaccuracies.

Thank you very much for reading this book.

Title: Hardwood Heroes
Subtitle: The Inside Story of 10 Iconic NBA Movies That Changed Basketball and Cinema

Author: Sophia M. Johnson

Epic Runtime Allows Thorough Look at Challenges and Inequity 232
Critically Lauded as a Work of Social Commentary 236
Influential Depiction of NBA Aspirations and Reality 240

Chapter 11 - Hardwood Themes: Comparing Cinematic Depictions 245
Varied Representations of Race, Gender, and Culture.......... 245
Characters United by Hoop Dreams and Obstacles.............. 249
Examining Narrative Tropes Across Genres........................ 254
Evolution of Basketball's Depiction Over the Decades 258

Chapter 12 - The Wider Influence of these NBA Films 262
Catchphrases, Soundtracks, and Iconic Scenes 262
Reflecting and Shaping the League's Personas and Stories. 266
Cementing Moments and Figures in Basketball Lore 270
Broadening Hoops' Reach Beyond the Hardwood................ 274

Conclusion - The Final Starting Five and Bench 278
Definitive Ranking of the 10 Most Significant NBA Films ... 278
Debating Snubs and Future Contenders 283
The Ever-Expanding Interplay of Hoops and Hollywood ... 287

Glossary.. 291
Potential References 294

Introduction
The Evolution of Hoop Dreams on the Big Screen

The court and the silver screen, seemingly distant realms, converge in a symphony of storytelling and competition. In "Hardwood Heroes: The Inside Story of 10 Iconic NBA Movies That Changed Basketball and Cinema," we embark on a journey through the annals of cinematic history, exploring the evolution of hoop dreams on the big screen. This introductory chapter sets the stage for a riveting exploration of how the art of filmmaking has intertwined with the passion and drama of basketball, creating a cultural phenomenon that transcends both courtside and theater seats.

The Intersection of Sport and Cinema: A Historical Prelude

The love affair between sports and cinema is not a recent phenomenon. From the early days of silent films to the technicolor extravaganzas of the mid-20th century, filmmakers have sought inspiration from the drama, heroics, and unscripted narratives of athletic pursuits. However, it was in the latter half of the 20th century that the marriage of basketball and cinema truly blossomed into an enduring and influential partnership.

Basketball, with its fast-paced action, high-flying dunks, and nail-biting buzzer-beaters, proved to be a captivating muse for filmmakers. The courtside became a stage, and the players became actors in a larger-than-life drama that unfolded before the eyes of eager audiences. As the sport gained popularity, so did the desire to capture its essence on film.

From Documentaries to Blockbusters: A Cinematic Evolution

The evolution of hoop dreams on the big screen is marked by a transition from early documentary-style narratives to mainstream blockbusters that seamlessly blend the sport's intensity with compelling storytelling. Documentaries like "Hoop Dreams" (1994) paved the way for a more authentic and unfiltered look at the lives of aspiring basketball players, revealing the triumphs and tribulations that transcended the game itself.

As the years rolled on, Hollywood recognized the cinematic potential in the hardwood tales of triumph and defeat. This transition is evident in the selection of our ten pivotal NBA films, each contributing a unique chapter to the evolving narrative of basketball cinema. These films not only entertained but also acted as cultural touchstones, shaping the way audiences perceived the sport and its larger-than-life protagonists.

Beyond the Highlight Reel: Exploring Themes and Narratives

Beyond the slam dunks and buzzer-beaters, basketball cinema became a canvas for exploring complex themes – race, class, love, and the pursuit of dreams. The court became a microcosm of society, reflecting and challenging prevailing norms and perceptions. Our exploration will delve into how each film tackled these themes, providing nuanced perspectives that transcended the confines of the basketball court.

The Cinematic Hoop Dreams Zeitgeist

The concept of "hoop dreams" is not confined to the realm of sports; it has become a cultural touchstone representing the pursuit of aspirations against all odds. In this cinematic journey, we will witness the evolution of this zeitgeist, from the early depictions of raw ambition in "Hoop Dreams" to the fantastical realms of "Space Jam." The intersection of dreams and reality, the personal and the collective, creates a tapestry that defines the essence of basketball cinema.

Our Cinematic Roster: The Chosen Ten

Before we delve into the individual narratives of our selected films, it's essential to understand the meticulous process of choosing these ten cinematic gems. From the iconic "Space Jam" to the groundbreaking "Hoop Dreams," each film on our roster played a pivotal role in shaping the landscape of basketball cinema. "Mapping the Game Plan: An Inside Look at the Films Chosen" will illuminate the criteria and considerations that led to the selection of these films, setting the stage for a deep dive into each cinematic masterpiece.

Join us as we dribble through time and celluloid, exploring the synergy between hardwood heroes and the storytellers who immortalized them on screen. The evolution of hoop dreams on the big screen is a tale as riveting as any buzzer-beater, and in the pages that follow, we invite you to witness the magic unfold, one frame at a time.

Selecting Cinema's 10 Most Pivotal Productions

As we embark on the cinematic journey chronicled in "Hardwood Heroes: The Inside Story of 10 Iconic NBA Movies That Changed Basketball and Cinema," the process of selecting the ten pivotal productions that grace our spotlight becomes a tale in itself. In this chapter, we unveil the meticulous criteria and considerations that guided the curation of cinema's most influential basketball narratives. "Selecting Cinema's 10 Most Pivotal Productions" lays bare the method behind the magic, revealing the delicate dance of storytelling, cultural impact, and cinematic excellence that defined our chosen roster.

The Art of Curation: Crafting a Cinematic Roster

Choosing the ten films that would embody the spirit and impact of basketball cinema proved to be a challenge laden with both excitement and responsibility. Our goal was not merely to assemble a list of box office hits or critically acclaimed movies but to curate a collection that collectively shaped and reflected the evolving narrative of the sport. Each film on our roster is a piece of the larger puzzle, contributing a unique perspective to the rich tapestry of basketball storytelling.

Criteria for Inclusion: Beyond Box Office Success

To ensure the diversity and depth of our cinematic roster, we applied a multifaceted set of criteria. Box office success, while a factor, was not the sole determinant. We sought films that left an indelible mark on both the sports and cinematic landscapes, movies that transcended their release dates to become timeless representations of the interplay between basketball and storytelling.

The cultural impact of each film was another crucial consideration. Did the movie resonate beyond the court and the theater, influencing the way society viewed the sport and its athletes? We delved into the annals of pop culture to gauge the lasting imprint of each production, from catchphrases that became part of everyday vernacular to iconic scenes etched into the collective memory of basketball enthusiasts.

Balancing Eras and Genres: A Chronological Tapestry

Our cinematic journey spans decades, from the black-and-white charm of "Hoosiers" to the high-flying fantasy of "Space Jam." Balancing eras allowed us to capture the evolution of basketball cinema, showcasing how storytelling techniques, societal themes, and the very nature of the sport underwent transformation over time. This chronological approach ensures that readers traverse the cinematic hardwood not only as spectators but as time travelers, witnessing the evolution of both cinema and basketball.

Genres, too, played a pivotal role in our selection. From documentaries to comedies, dramas to fantasies, each genre brought a unique flavor to the basketball narrative. "Selecting Cinema's 10 Most Pivotal Productions" explores how the fusion of genres contributed to the richness and versatility of the selected films, offering audiences varied perspectives on the sport and its cultural significance.

Beyond Hollywood: Global Perspectives and Influence

While Hollywood has been a significant contributor to basketball cinema, our curation extends beyond the borders of the United States. The global appeal of basketball has been mirrored in international productions that captured the essence of the sport from diverse cultural perspectives. In this chapter, we shed light on how films like "Hoop Dreams" and "Space Jam" transcended national boundaries, becoming touchstones for basketball enthusiasts worldwide.

Unveiling the Chosen Ten: A Sneak Peek

Before we delve into the intricacies of each film, "Selecting Cinema's 10 Most Pivotal Productions" provides readers with a sneak peek into the chosen ten. A brief overview of each movie sets the stage for the deep exploration that follows, offering a taste of the narratives, themes, and cinematic techniques that make these films stand out in the illustrious realm of basketball cinema.

Join us as we pull back the curtain on the thought process that went into crafting this cinematic lineup. The stage is set, the lights are dimmed, and our chosen ten await their moment in the spotlight. Let the cinematic journey begin.

Mapping the Game Plan: An Inside Look at the Films Chosen

As we navigate the cinematic landscape in "Hardwood Heroes: The Inside Story of 10 Iconic NBA Movies That Changed Basketball and Cinema," our journey extends beyond the silver screen to the meticulous process of selecting and organizing the chosen films. In "Mapping the Game Plan: An Inside Look at the Films Chosen," we unveil the strategic decisions, thematic considerations, and cinematic nuances that guided the placement of each production within the narrative arc of our exploration. This chapter serves as a roadmap, inviting readers into the intricate choreography of storytelling that defines our cinematic lineup.

The Unseen Draft: Behind-the-Scenes Selection Process

Before the lights dimmed and the cameras rolled, the selection process for our ten pivotal productions unfolded like an unseen draft. The task of choosing films that encapsulated the essence of basketball cinema required a delicate balance of thematic diversity, cultural impact, and cinematic prowess. "Mapping the Game Plan" provides readers with a backstage pass, offering insights into the discussions, debates, and, at times, the impassioned advocacy that characterized the curation process.

Delving into the decision-making matrix, we explore how each film earned its place on our roster. From the emotional resonance of "Hoosiers" to the cultural phenomenon of "Space Jam," the films chosen are not merely a random assortment but a carefully crafted ensemble that collectively paints a comprehensive portrait of basketball on the big screen.

Thematic Threads: Connecting the Cinematic Dots

As we unveil the films chosen, readers will witness the deliberate threading of thematic connections that weave through the narrative fabric. Beyond chronological placement, thematic threads form an integral part of our game plan. Whether exploring the underdog narrative in "Hoosiers" or the fantastical realms of "Space Jam," each film resonates with others, creating a seamless flow that transcends individual plots to tell a larger, interconnected story.

"Mapping the Game Plan" delves into the thematic considerations that guided our choices, providing readers with a deeper understanding of how these films complement and contrast, forming a tapestry that celebrates the diversity and complexity of basketball cinema.

From Documentaries to Blockbusters: Crafting a Cinematic Spectrum

Our game plan extends beyond thematic considerations to encompass a cinematic spectrum that spans genres and styles. From the raw authenticity of documentaries like "Hoop Dreams" to the high-octane spectacle of blockbuster fantasies like "Space Jam," our selection embraces the full range of storytelling possibilities. "Mapping the Game Plan" sheds light on how this intentional spectrum enriches the reader's experience, offering a well-rounded exploration of basketball cinema's diverse expressions.

Cinematic Milestones: Placing Films in Cultural Context

Placing each film within its cultural context is crucial to understanding its impact and relevance. "Mapping the Game Plan" takes readers on a journey through the cultural milestones represented by each film. Whether capturing the zeitgeist of the '90s in "White Men Can't Jump" or challenging racial norms in "Glory Road," our lineup serves as a chronicle of not only basketball history but also the broader cultural landscape that shaped these cinematic gems.

Strategic Arrangement: The Dance of Chronology

Beyond thematic threads and cultural contexts, "Mapping the Game Plan" explores the deliberate choreography of chronological arrangement. Each film is a chapter in the larger narrative of basketball cinema, contributing to the evolving story of the sport on the big screen. From the nostalgia of '80s classics to the modern complexities of the 21st century, our arrangement offers readers a temporal journey through the evolution of basketball storytelling.

Building Anticipation: A Preview of Films to Come

Before we embark on the individual explorations of each film, "Mapping the Game Plan" builds anticipation by providing a preview of the cinematic treasures that lie ahead. This sneak peek offers glimpses into the narratives, characters, and cinematic techniques that define our chosen ten, setting the stage for a deep dive into the heart of basketball cinema.

Join us as we unfold the game plan, revealing the intricate strategy that guides our exploration. The court is set, the players are in position, and the cinematic journey is about to unfold. Let the game plan unravel, frame by frame, as we navigate the world of "Hardwood Heroes."

Chapter 1 - Space Jam (1996)
Spinning a Hollywood Fantasy Starring Michael Jordan

As we step onto the hardwood court of cinematic history, our journey begins with the fantastical slam dunk that is "Space Jam" (1996). In this chapter, we unravel the magic behind the creation of this iconic film, exploring how it spun a Hollywood fantasy starring none other than the basketball legend himself, Michael Jordan.

The Genesis of a Cosmic Concept: Merging Animation and Live-Action

"Space Jam" didn't just break the mold; it shattered expectations by merging the animated world of Looney Tunes with live-action sequences. The idea of bringing together Michael Jordan, the towering titan of basketball, and the whimsical, animated characters of the Looney Tunes universe was a cosmic concept that sparked both curiosity and skepticism. In "Spinning a Hollywood Fantasy Starring Michael Jordan," we delve into the genesis of this audacious idea, exploring how the film's creators navigated the uncharted territory of blending real-life sports superstardom with animated antics.

The synergy between animation and live-action proved to be a stroke of genius, offering audiences a surreal, yet captivating, cinematic experience. Michael Jordan's larger-than-life presence seamlessly interwoven with Bugs Bunny, Daffy Duck, and the rest of the Looney Tunes cast created a spectacle that transcended the boundaries of traditional storytelling.

Behind the Scenes: The Michael Jordan Effect

While the concept was ambitious, the execution required a star who could not only hold his own on the basketball court but also navigate the nuanced interplay between reality and animation. Enter Michael Jordan, whose impact on the film extended far beyond his slam dunks and three-pointers.

"Spinning a Hollywood Fantasy Starring Michael Jordan" takes readers behind the scenes, exploring the synergy between Jordan's magnetic charisma and the animated world he found himself in. From his on-set interactions with animated co-stars to the challenges of acting alongside characters added in post-production, the chapter sheds light on how Jordan's natural charm and athleticism elevated the film from a mere crossover experiment to a cinematic phenomenon.

From Courtside to Soundstage: Crafting the Basketball Sequences

One of the film's highlights is undoubtedly the incorporation of high-stakes basketball games into the storyline. In this chapter, we dissect how the filmmakers seamlessly integrated live-action basketball sequences with animated characters, creating an electrifying spectacle that captivated audiences. From choreographing the dynamic plays to capturing the essence of Jordan's legendary skills, "Spinning a Hollywood Fantasy Starring Michael Jordan" offers an in-depth look at the craftsmanship that went into bringing the basketball court to life on the big screen.

Global Stardom and Brand Power: The Michael Jordan Phenomenon

As we explore the film's impact, it's essential to recognize the unique cultural moment in which "Space Jam" emerged. Michael Jordan wasn't just a basketball player; he was a global icon, a brand unto himself. "Spinning a Hollywood Fantasy Starring Michael Jordan" examines how the film leveraged Jordan's unparalleled stardom to create a cinematic event that resonated far beyond the basketball community.

The synergy between Jordan's on-court prowess and his off-court charisma transformed "Space Jam" into more than just a movie; it became a cultural phenomenon. From the iconic soundtrack featuring the Quad City DJ's hit "Space Jam" to the Air Jordan sneakers that transcended the court and became a fashion statement, the chapter explores how the film added another layer to the Michael Jordan legend.

Commercial Success and Enduring Pop Culture Impact

Box office numbers tell only part of the story. "Spinning a Hollywood Fantasy Starring Michael Jordan" delves into the commercial success of "Space Jam" and its enduring impact on pop culture. The film's reach extended beyond theaters, influencing merchandise, video games, and even inspiring a new generation of basketball enthusiasts. Through interviews, box office data, and cultural analysis, the chapter unpacks how "Space Jam" became a lasting cultural touchstone, leaving an indelible mark on the intersection of sports and entertainment.

As we lace up our sneakers and step onto the court of imagination, "Spinning a Hollywood Fantasy Starring Michael Jordan" invites readers to relive the magic of "Space Jam" and understand the alchemy that transformed a seemingly unconventional idea into a timeless cinematic classic. The chapter pays homage to the film that set the stage for our exploration of basketball cinema, celebrating the synergy between the earthly prowess of Michael Jordan and the whimsical charm of the Looney Tunes universe.

Blending Live-Action with Beloved Looney Tunes Characters

In the realm where the court meets the cartoon, "Space Jam" (1996) orchestrated a symphony of sports and animation, forever etching its place in the annals of cinematic history. In this chapter, we embark on a journey through the cosmic collaboration that brought beloved Looney Tunes characters to life alongside live-action sequences, exploring the ingenious alchemy that birthed a cinematic universe where reality and animation seamlessly coexist.

The Looney Tunes Renaissance: A Leap from Small to Big Screen

Before "Space Jam," the Looney Tunes characters were animated staples, entertaining audiences on the small screen. However, with the audacious move to blend these beloved characters with live-action elements, the film not only brought Bugs Bunny, Daffy Duck, and company to a new generation but also catapulted them onto the silver screen in a way never before imagined.

This section delves into the decision to elevate these animated icons into a live-action setting, exploring the creative risks and rewards that came with the ambitious endeavor. By examining the history and cultural impact of the Looney Tunes characters, we contextualize their transition from Saturday morning cartoons to cinematic superstardom.

Crafting a Seamless Fusion: The Technical Marvels of Animation

Bringing animated characters into the live-action realm posed a myriad of technical challenges, and "Space Jam" rose to meet them head-on. "Blending Live-Action with Beloved Looney Tunes Characters" unravels the technical wizardry behind the film, from the pioneering use of green screens to the intricacies of integrating 2D animated characters with 3D live-action environments.

Interviews with the animators, visual effects artists, and directors involved provide insights into the innovative techniques employed to create a seamless fusion of worlds. This section celebrates the technical achievements that allowed Bugs Bunny to share the screen with Michael Jordan and Daffy Duck to interact with Bill Murray, transcending the boundaries between reality and animation.

The Animation Dream Team: Looney Tunes Meet NBA Superstars

One of the film's unique draws was the convergence of the Looney Tunes ensemble with real-life NBA superstars. "Blending Live-Action with Beloved Looney Tunes Characters" explores the dynamic between animated mischief-makers and basketball titans, delving into how the film harnessed the larger-than-life personas of both to create a spectacle that appealed to audiences across demographics.

The chapter sheds light on the collaborative process between animators and athletes, detailing how the animated characters were tailored to complement the playing styles and personalities of NBA stars. From Michael Jordan's slam dunks to Charles Barkley's animated alter ego, the synergy between live-action and animation allowed the Looney Tunes to weave seamlessly into the narrative tapestry of basketball.

Challenges and Triumphs: Navigating the Hybrid Landscape

As groundbreaking as the concept was, blending live-action and animation came with its share of challenges. "Blending Live-Action with Beloved Looney Tunes Characters" doesn't shy away from exploring the obstacles faced during production, from the complexities of coordinating live-action performances with animated characters to the meticulous planning required to ensure a cohesive visual narrative.

By highlighting these challenges, the chapter provides a nuanced understanding of the filmmaking process, acknowledging the risks taken to deliver a cinematic experience that defied conventions. It also celebrates the triumphs that emerged from the collaborative efforts of a dedicated team determined to bring the Looney Tunes to life in a way that had never been attempted before.

The Cinematic Playground: Interactions and Dynamics

"Space Jam" not only brought Looney Tunes characters into the real world but also showcased their interactions with live-action counterparts. This section explores the dynamics between animated and live-action characters, from the comedic banter between Bugs Bunny and Daffy Duck to the surprising cameos by Bill Murray and Wayne Knight.

Through scene analysis and behind-the-scenes anecdotes, "Blending Live-Action with Beloved Looney Tunes Characters" unveils the playful chemistry that defined the on-screen relationships. The cinematic playground becomes a stage where cartoon antics meld with real-world humor, offering audiences a delightful and unpredictable journey through a universe where anything is possible.

The Legacy of Animation Integration: Impact on Filmmaking

The success of "Space Jam" reverberated beyond its initial release, leaving a lasting impact on the way filmmakers approached the integration of animation with live-action. "Blending Live-Action with Beloved Looney Tunes Characters" examines the legacy of the film, tracing its influence on subsequent productions and the evolution of animation techniques in cinema.

Through interviews with filmmakers and industry experts, the chapter explores how "Space Jam" became a touchstone for the seamless integration of animated characters into live-action narratives, setting a precedent for future films that would explore similar creative terrain.

From the Drawing Board to the Big Screen: A Cinematic Triumph

As we conclude our exploration of the fusion between live-action and animated worlds in "Space Jam," it becomes evident that the film's success lies not just in its star-studded cast or imaginative storyline but in the bold decision to blend reality with fantasy. "Blending Live-Action with Beloved Looney Tunes Characters" serves as a testament to the cinematic triumph achieved by bringing iconic animated characters out of the drawing board and into the dynamic landscape of live-action cinema.

The chapter invites readers to appreciate the intricacies of this groundbreaking cinematic experiment, celebrating the harmonious blend of live-action and animation that transformed "Space Jam" into a cultural phenomenon. From the technical marvels that brought Bugs and his pals to life to the collaborative dance between NBA superstars and animated mischief-makers, this section unfolds the behind-the-scenes magic that turned a seemingly improbable concept into a timeless classic.

Commercial Success and Enduring Pop Culture Impact

As we traverse the courts of celluloid history in "Hardwood Heroes: The Inside Story of 10 Iconic NBA Movies That Changed Basketball and Cinema," our journey commences with the meteoric rise of "Space Jam" (1996). This chapter peels back the layers of its commercial success and enduring pop culture impact, exploring how a film that blended live-action with animated antics became more than just a box office triumph; it became a cultural touchstone that resonates to this day.

Box Office Slam Dunk: The Economic Triumph of "Space Jam"

"Space Jam" wasn't just a film; it was an event that captured the imagination of audiences worldwide. As we delve into its commercial success, we witness the film's journey from an audacious experiment to a bona fide box office slam dunk. Through interviews with industry experts, box office analyses, and contemporary reviews, we unpack the economic triumph that turned "Space Jam" into a cinematic phenomenon.

The chapter navigates the film's journey from pre-release skepticism to post-release adulation, exploring how the synergy between live-action, animation, and the star power of Michael Jordan propelled it into the stratosphere of commercial success. From its opening weekend to its international reception, "Commercial Success and Enduring Pop Culture Impact" provides a comprehensive look at the economic dimensions of the film's triumph.

Beyond the Screen: Merchandising, Soundtracks, and More

The impact of "Space Jam" extended far beyond the confines of the movie theater. This section explores the sprawling world of merchandising that accompanied the film's release, from T-shirts and toys to lunchboxes and video games. "Commercial Success and Enduring Pop Culture Impact" dissects how the Looney Tunes characters, now infused with the magic of Michael Jordan, became cultural icons in their own right, adorning everything from apparel to school supplies.

Additionally, the film's soundtrack, featuring tracks like "I Believe I Can Fly" by R. Kelly and the infectious "Space Jam" by the Quad City DJ's, soared on music charts and became an integral part of the film's legacy. This chapter delves into the symbiotic relationship between the film and its soundtrack, exploring how the music became a cultural force in its own right.

The Michael Jordan Brand: A Cinematic Catalyst

Michael Jordan wasn't just a basketball player; he was a global brand, and "Space Jam" served as a cinematic catalyst that further elevated his iconic status. "Commercial Success and Enduring Pop Culture Impact" explores the intersection of sports and marketing, examining how the film contributed to the perpetuation of the Jordan brand.

Through advertisements, endorsements, and the strategic alignment of the Air Jordan line with the film, the chapter unfolds the marketing strategies that transformed "Space Jam" into a vehicle for extending Jordan's influence beyond the basketball court. We explore how the film became a powerful tool in shaping the narrative of Jordan as not just an athlete but a cultural icon.

From Nostalgia to New Generations: Enduring Pop Culture Impact

Decades after its release, "Space Jam" continues to resonate in the collective memory of audiences. This section investigates the enduring pop culture impact of the film, examining how it has become a nostalgic touchstone for those who grew up in the '90s. Through interviews with fans, cultural critics, and contemporary analyses, the chapter unpacks the reasons behind the film's enduring popularity.

Furthermore, we explore how "Space Jam" has transcended generational boundaries, captivating new audiences who were not around during its initial release. From memes and social media references to the anticipation surrounding the sequel, "Commercial Success and Enduring Pop Culture Impact" examines how "Space Jam" has cemented its place in the pantheon of enduring pop culture phenomena.

Critics vs. Audience: A Cultural Divide

While the film achieved commercial success and enduring popularity, it wasn't without its share of critical scrutiny. "Commercial Success and Enduring Pop Culture Impact" navigates the divide between critical reviews and audience reception, unpacking the reasons behind the disparity. By exploring contemporary critiques and retrospectives, the chapter provides a nuanced understanding of how "Space Jam" became a cultural touchstone despite, and perhaps because of, its polarizing reception among critics.

Legacy Beyond the Court: A Cultural Time Capsule

As we conclude our exploration of the commercial success and enduring pop culture impact of "Space Jam," it becomes evident that the film is not merely a cinematic relic of the '90s; it is a cultural time capsule that encapsulates the spirit of an era. From its economic triumphs to its lasting influence on merchandise, marketing, and music, "Commercial Success and Enduring Pop Culture Impact" unravels the layers that have contributed to the film's enduring legacy.

The chapter invites readers to reflect on the multifaceted impact of "Space Jam," from its role in shaping the Michael Jordan brand to its status as a nostalgic cornerstone for multiple generations. In doing so, it sets the stage for our broader exploration of basketball cinema, illustrating how a seemingly unconventional film can transcend its initial reception to become an enduring cultural phenomenon.

The Peak of Jordan's Global Stardom and Brand Power

In the storied career of Michael Jordan, "Space Jam" stands as a unique chapter that catapulted the basketball legend to the zenith of global stardom and brand power. This chapter delves into the cosmic convergence of sports and entertainment, exploring how "Space Jam" became the apex of Jordan's influence, transforming him from a sports icon into a global brand.

The Michael Jordan Phenomenon: From Courtside to Worldwide

Long before "Space Jam," Michael Jordan had transcended the confines of basketball courts to become a global phenomenon. His prowess on the hardwood had already secured his status as one of the greatest basketball players of all time, but "Space Jam" would elevate him to a new stratosphere of fame. This section explores the cultural landscape that defined the Michael Jordan phenomenon leading up to the film's release.

Through archival footage, interviews, and cultural analyses, we unravel the magnetic charisma and athletic brilliance that made Jordan not just an athlete but a cultural symbol. From the Air Jordan sneaker craze to his magnetic presence in advertising campaigns, we set the stage for how "Space Jam" would further amplify the Michael Jordan mystique on a global scale.

The Unlikely Crossover: Michael Jordan Meets Bugs Bunny

"Space Jam" emerged as an unlikely crossover, blending the worlds of professional basketball and animated antics. For Michael Jordan, this was not just a film; it was a venture into uncharted territory, a testament to his willingness to embrace the unexpected. This section explores the decision-making process that led to Jordan's involvement in the film and the potential risks and rewards associated with merging his athletic persona with the whimsical world of Looney Tunes.

Through interviews with Jordan himself, as well as key members of the production team, we gain insights into how the crossover concept unfolded. It became more than just a movie; it became a defining moment where the lines between sports and entertainment blurred, propelling Jordan into a new realm of cultural relevance.

Brand Jordan: The Intersection of Sports and Marketing

As the film's production unfolded, the synergy between Michael Jordan and the Looney Tunes characters became a metaphorical slam dunk for marketing. This section delves into the strategic decisions that transformed "Space Jam" into a powerful branding tool, extending the Jordan brand beyond the basketball court.

From the strategic placement of Air Jordan sneakers in the film to the creation of iconic merchandise, "The Peak of Jordan's Global Stardom and Brand Power" examines how the film became a nexus where sports and marketing converged. Interviews with marketing experts shed light on the deliberate choices made to solidify Jordan's image not just as a basketball player but as a lifestyle brand.

Air Jordan Takes Flight: Sneaker Culture and Beyond

The Air Jordan sneaker line had already become a cultural phenomenon by the time "Space Jam" was in development, but the film added a new dimension to sneaker culture. This section explores the symbiotic relationship between the film and the Air Jordan brand, unraveling how the iconic sneakers became not just athletic wear but a symbol of cultural coolness.

Through discussions with sneaker enthusiasts, fashion experts, and industry insiders, we dissect the impact of the Air Jordan sneakers featured in "Space Jam." The chapter also explores the lasting legacy of the sneakers, examining how they continue to be coveted by collectors and sneakerheads around the world.

From Courts to Commercials: Expanding the Jordan Brand

"Space Jam" wasn't just a cinematic venture; it was a strategic expansion of the Jordan brand into the realms of entertainment and popular culture. This section navigates the commercials and promotional campaigns that accompanied the film, exploring how they reinforced the narrative of Michael Jordan as a global icon.

Interviews with advertising executives and cultural critics shed light on the impact of these campaigns, dissecting how they contributed to the evolution of the Jordan brand. The chapter unravels the storytelling techniques used in commercials, illustrating how they became a narrative extension of the cinematic universe created by "Space Jam."

Global Stardom: The Film's Contribution to Jordan's Persona

As "Space Jam" hit theaters, Michael Jordan's global stardom reached unprecedented heights. This section explores the reception of the film on the international stage and its contribution to Jordan's persona as a global cultural icon.

Through audience reactions, media coverage, and interviews with international fans, we unveil how "Space Jam" resonated beyond American borders. The chapter also examines how the film's success opened new doors for Jordan in international markets, shaping perceptions of him as not just an athlete but a transcendent figure with universal appeal.

The Celebrity Cameos: NBA Stars and Hollywood Icons

Beyond Michael Jordan, "Space Jam" featured a roster of NBA stars and Hollywood icons. This section explores the impact of these celebrity cameos on the film's overall narrative and, by extension, on Jordan's global stardom.

From Charles Barkley's animated alter ego to the unexpected presence of Bill Murray and Wayne Knight, the chapter dissects how these cameos contributed to the film's charm and cultural significance. Interviews with the supporting cast provide insights into the collaborative spirit that defined the production and how these celebrity interactions further solidified Jordan's status as a cultural linchpin.

The Legacy of "Space Jam": A Cultural Time Capsule

As we conclude our exploration of "The Peak of Jordan's Global Stardom and Brand Power," it becomes evident that "Space Jam" was not just a film; it was a cultural time capsule that encapsulated the essence of Michael Jordan's ascendancy to global stardom. From the strategic branding decisions to the film's reception on the international stage, this chapter illuminates the multifaceted layers that contributed to the peak of Jordan's influence.

The chapter invites readers to reflect on how "Space Jam" served as a pivotal moment in the intersection of sports, entertainment, and marketing, reshaping the narrative around Michael Jordan. As we step beyond the celluloid frames of the film, we carry with us the enduring legacy of "Space Jam," a legacy that continues to echo in the realms of sports, branding, and global popular culture.

Chapter 2 - Hoosiers (1986)
Bringing the True Story of the Milan Miracle to Screen

In the heartland of Indiana, "Hoosiers" (1986) emerged as more than a basketball film; it became a cinematic ode to the resilience of the human spirit and a tribute to the transformative power of the game. This chapter delves into the creation of "Hoosiers," exploring the delicate task of bringing the true story of the Milan Miracle to the screen and the profound impact it had on both the sports movie genre and the cultural understanding of small-town basketball.

The Milan Miracle: A Tale of Triumph Against Odds

At the core of "Hoosiers" lies the inspiring narrative of the Milan Miracle, a real-life story of a small-town high school basketball team that defied all odds to become state champions in 1954. "Bringing the True Story of the Milan Miracle to Screen" begins by unraveling the historical context and significance of the Milan Miracle, setting the stage for how this underdog story captivated the imagination of audiences and filmmakers alike.

Through interviews with key figures involved in the Milan Miracle, archival footage, and contemporary reflections, we provide a comprehensive understanding of the events that inspired the film. The chapter navigates the cultural landscape of 1950s Indiana, exploring the fervor surrounding high school basketball and the tight-knit communities that rallied behind their local teams.

Screenwriting Alchemy: Crafting the Hoosiers Narrative

Bringing the Milan Miracle to the screen required a delicate balance between historical accuracy and cinematic storytelling. This section dissects the screenwriting alchemy that transformed the true events into a compelling narrative, exploring the decisions made to capture the essence of the story while adapting it to the language of cinema.

Through interviews with screenwriter Angelo Pizzo and director David Anspaugh, we gain insights into the creative choices that shaped the screenplay. The chapter delves into the challenges of condensing a real-life season into a feature-length film and examines how the characters were developed to convey the emotional stakes of the Milan Miracle.

Casting the Hoosiers: Translating History into Performances

The success of "Hoosiers" hinged on more than just a faithful script; it required performances that could breathe life into the characters inspired by real people. "Bringing the True Story of the Milan Miracle to Screen" explores the casting process, unraveling how actors like Gene Hackman, Dennis Hopper, and the ensemble of young athletes were chosen to embody the spirit of the Milan team.

Through interviews with the cast, casting directors, and the creative team, the chapter delves into the transformational journey of actors as they stepped into the shoes of real-life individuals. From capturing the coaching demeanor of Norman Dale (played by Hackman) to embodying the struggles and triumphs of Jimmy Chitwood (played by Maris Valainis), we uncover the intricate process of translating historical figures into unforgettable on-screen performances.

Small Town, Big Emotions: Filming on Location in Indiana

To authentically capture the essence of small-town Indiana and the fervor of high school basketball, "Hoosiers" was filmed on location in various towns, including the actual site of the Milan Miracle. This section explores the decision to film in Indiana, providing a behind-the-scenes look at the challenges and rewards of immersing the production in the real-life communities that inspired the story.

Through interviews with the filmmakers, locals, and members of the Milan High School community, we uncover the impact of filming on location. The chapter navigates the collaborative spirit between the filmmakers and the residents, examining how this synergy contributed to the authenticity and emotional resonance of the film.

From the Court to the Screen: Capturing Basketball Realism

"Hoosiers" set a standard for realistic basketball depictions in cinema, capturing the intensity, strategy, and raw emotion of the game. This section explores the commitment to basketball authenticity, examining how the filmmakers worked with the actors to bring a genuine portrayal of the sport to the screen.

Through interviews with basketball consultants, coaches, and the cast, we delve into the training regimen that prepared the actors for the court. The chapter dissects the cinematographic techniques employed to capture the dynamism of basketball, providing insights into the choreography and camera work that contributed to the film's reputation as one of the most realistic portrayals of the sport in cinematic history.

The Music of Hoosiers: Scoring Triumph and Emotion

The musical score of "Hoosiers" played a crucial role in enhancing the emotional impact of the film. This section explores the collaboration between composer Jerry Goldsmith and the filmmakers, unraveling how the musical score became a narrative force that underscored the triumphs and tribulations of the Milan team.

Through interviews with Goldsmith's collaborators and analyses of the score, the chapter delves into the compositional choices that elevated key moments in the film. From the soaring melodies that accompanied the team's victories to the poignant undertones in moments of struggle, we explore how the music became an integral part of the storytelling fabric.

Critical Reception and Cultural Impact: Hoosiers as a Cultural Touchstone

Upon its release, "Hoosiers" received critical acclaim for its authenticity, performances, and emotional resonance. This section navigates the critical reception, examining the reviews and accolades that celebrated the film as a cinematic triumph. Interviews with film critics provide insights into how "Hoosiers" was received within the context of sports cinema and the broader cultural landscape.

Beyond critical acclaim, the chapter explores the enduring cultural impact of "Hoosiers," which has solidified its status as a timeless classic. From its inclusion in sports movie retrospectives to its continued resonance among audiences, we uncover how the film has become a cultural touchstone that transcends the genre.

Legacy of the Milan Miracle: Beyond the Hoosiers Hype

As we conclude our exploration of "Bringing the True Story of the Milan Miracle to Screen," it becomes evident that "Hoosiers" was not merely a film about basketball; it was a cinematic canvas that painted a vivid portrait of human resilience, community spirit, and the transformative power of sports. The chapter invites readers to reflect on how the filmmakers delicately navigated the line between historical accuracy and cinematic storytelling, creating a film that remains a testament to the enduring legacy of the Milan Miracle and the small-town ethos that captivated audiences worldwide.

Gene Hackman Anchors the Underdog Sports Drama

In the expansive realm of sports cinema, "Hoosiers" (1986) stands as a beacon of the underdog sports drama, a testament to the enduring appeal of stories that transcend the court and delve into the human condition. At the heart of this cinematic triumph is the formidable presence of Gene Hackman, whose portrayal of Coach Norman Dale anchors the film's narrative and elevates it to the echelons of sports movie greatness. This chapter unpacks the nuanced performance of Hackman, exploring how his portrayal of Coach Dale became the linchpin of "Hoosiers" and contributed to the enduring legacy of the film.

Crafting Coach Norman Dale: The Complexity of Leadership

Gene Hackman's portrayal of Coach Norman Dale is a masterclass in character craftsmanship. This section delves into the intricacies of creating a character who embodies the complexities of leadership, discipline, and redemption. Through interviews with Hackman, director David Anspaugh, and screenwriter Angelo Pizzo, we gain insights into the collaborative process that shaped the character of Coach Dale.

The chapter explores how Hackman approached the role, drawing inspiration from real-life coaches and infusing the character with a blend of stern authority, vulnerability, and a genuine passion for the game. Through scene analyses and behind-the-scenes anecdotes, we unravel the layers that make Coach Dale more than a conventional sports movie archetype; he becomes a symbol of resilience and redemption.

From Maverick to Mentor: Coach Dale's Evolution

Coach Norman Dale's journey in "Hoosiers" is a narrative arc that transcends the boundaries of sports storytelling. This section traces the evolution of Coach Dale from a maverick figure with a controversial past to a mentor who guides his team to an improbable state championship. Through a close examination of key scenes, we dissect how Hackman navigates the emotional terrain of Coach Dale's character, portraying a man burdened by his own mistakes yet driven by a desire for redemption.

Interviews with the filmmakers shed light on the decision-making process that guided Coach Dale's character development. The chapter explores how Hackman's performance captures the internal conflicts of a coach seeking not just victory on the court but personal redemption in a small Indiana town.

Coach Dale and the Players: Navigating Team Dynamics

A hallmark of "Hoosiers" is the symbiotic relationship between Coach Dale and his players. This section delves into the dynamics of the coach-player relationships, exploring how Hackman navigates the nuances of mentorship, discipline, and camaraderie. Interviews with the young actors who portrayed the Hickory Huskers provide insights into the collaborative process that defined the on-screen chemistry.

Through scene analyses, we unravel how Hackman's interactions with characters like Jimmy Chitwood, played by Maris Valainis, and Shooter, portrayed by Dennis Hopper, contribute to the emotional resonance of the film. The chapter examines the delicate balance between authority and empathy that defines Coach Dale's coaching style, creating a dynamic that goes beyond the conventional sports movie coach-player dynamic.

The Coach's Philosophy: Basketball as a Metaphor for Life

"Hoosiers" elevates the game of basketball beyond the confines of the court, using it as a metaphor for life's challenges and triumphs. This section explores Coach Dale's coaching philosophy and how Hackman imbues the character with a deeper understanding of the game as a conduit for personal growth and community unity.

Through interviews with sports psychologists and basketball consultants who collaborated on the film, we dissect the elements of Coach Dale's coaching philosophy. The chapter navigates how Hackman's portrayal captures the transformative power of sports, illustrating how the game becomes a vehicle for self-discovery and communal bonding in the fictional town of Hickory.

The Moral Compass: Coach Dale's Ethical Dilemmas

Coach Norman Dale faces ethical dilemmas that transcend the realm of sports, adding layers of complexity to his character. This section explores how Hackman navigates the moral landscape of Coach Dale, examining pivotal moments where the coach must make decisions that go beyond the scoreboard.

Through scene analyses and interviews with the filmmakers, we unravel how Hackman's performance captures the internal struggles of a coach torn between personal convictions and the expectations of a community. The chapter delves into how these ethical dilemmas contribute to the richness of Coach Dale's character, making him a flawed yet empathetic protagonist.

Hackman on Set: The Actor's Craft and Collaboration

Gene Hackman's presence on the set of "Hoosiers" had a profound impact on the film's overall atmosphere and the performances of his co-stars. This section explores the actor's craft and collaborative spirit as he worked alongside a talented ensemble cast. Interviews with the cast and crew provide a behind-the-scenes look at the collaborative process and the influence of Hackman's seasoned presence.

The chapter examines how Hackman's approach to acting, including his interactions with fellow actors and the director, contributed to the authenticity and emotional depth of the film. From improvised moments to scripted dialogues, we unravel the alchemy that occurs when a seasoned actor of Hackman's caliber becomes the linchpin of a cinematic narrative.

Critical Acclaim and Awards: Gene Hackman's Impact

Upon the release of "Hoosiers," Gene Hackman's performance as Coach Norman Dale garnered widespread critical acclaim. This section delves into the reviews and accolades that celebrated Hackman's nuanced portrayal, examining how the actor's commitment to the role contributed to the film's success.

Through interviews with film critics and industry insiders, we navigate the impact of Hackman's performance on the reception of "Hoosiers" within the context of sports cinema. The chapter also explores the awards and nominations that followed, underscoring how Hackman's portrayal became a pivotal factor in the film's recognition as a cinematic triumph.

Legacy of Coach Norman Dale: Beyond the Final Buzzer

As we conclude our exploration of "Gene Hackman Anchors the Underdog Sports Drama," it becomes evident that Coach Norman Dale is more than just a cinematic character; he is an enduring symbol of resilience, redemption, and the transformative power of sports. The chapter invites readers to reflect on how Gene Hackman's portrayal elevated "Hoosiers" beyond the realm of sports movie conventions, creating a timeless narrative that resonates with audiences far beyond the final buzzer. Coach Norman Dale, brought to life by Hackman's masterful performance, stands as a testament to the enduring impact of well-crafted characters in the realm of sports cinema.

Capturing the Magic of Indiana High School Hoops

In the sprawling tapestry of American basketball lore, few stories resonate as profoundly as the magic of Indiana high school hoops. "Hoosiers" (1986) emerges as a cinematic vessel that captures not just the game itself but the spirit of a community bound together by a shared passion for basketball. This chapter delves into the film's portrayal of the enchanting world of Indiana high school basketball, exploring how "Hoosiers" became a love letter to the sport's grassroots and an embodiment of the state's basketball obsession.

The Heartbeat of Hoosier Hysteria: Indiana's Basketball Culture

"Hoosiers" doesn't merely unfold against the backdrop of Indiana's basketball culture; it immerses itself in the very heartbeat of Hoosier Hysteria. This section unravels the cultural significance of high school basketball in Indiana, setting the stage for understanding how the film taps into a collective love affair with the sport.

Through interviews with basketball historians, Indiana natives, and cultural analysts, the chapter navigates the origins of Hoosier Hysteria and its evolution into a cultural phenomenon. From the small-town gyms to the statewide tournaments, we explore how basketball transcended being a mere sport to become an intrinsic part of Indiana's identity.

Small Towns, Big Dreams: The Setting of Hickory

The fictional town of Hickory becomes more than just a backdrop; it becomes a character in itself, embodying the quintessential small-town ethos of Indiana. This section delves into how the filmmakers meticulously crafted the setting to capture the essence of Indiana's rural landscape and the intimate connection between the community and its high school basketball team.

Through interviews with production designers and location scouts, we unravel the decisions that went into creating the visual authenticity of Hickory. From the weathered barns to the dimly lit gyms, the chapter explores how the setting becomes a visual metaphor for the simplicity, resilience, and interconnectedness of small-town life.

The Rhythms of Hoosier High School Basketball: Authenticity in Action

"Hoosiers" achieves a rare feat in sports cinema: it authentically captures the rhythms of high school basketball, from the pre-game rituals to the frenetic energy on the court. This section delves into the meticulous attention to detail that went into recreating the authenticity of Indiana high school hoops, exploring how the filmmakers worked to ensure that every bounce of the ball echoed the spirit of the game.

Through interviews with basketball consultants, players, and the cast, the chapter navigates the behind-the-scenes efforts to achieve basketball realism. From choreographing plays to replicating the energy of a packed gym, we unravel the commitment to authenticity that defines the film's portrayal of the magic of Indiana high school basketball.

The Coach and the Community: A Symbiotic Relationship

In Indiana, the coach of a high school basketball team is more than a strategist; they are a community leader, a mentor, and a symbol of hope. This section explores how "Hoosiers" encapsulates the symbiotic relationship between the coach and the community, emphasizing the role of Coach Norman Dale as a unifying force in the town of Hickory.

Through interviews with the filmmakers and basketball experts, the chapter delves into the real-life inspirations for Coach Dale and how his character embodies the archetypal high school basketball coach in Indiana. The chapter also explores the broader theme of community support, showcasing how the film portrays the interconnectedness between the team's success and the town's collective spirit.

Pinnacle of Hoosier Hoops: The State Basketball Tournament

The pinnacle of Indiana high school basketball is the state tournament, a spectacle that transcends the boundaries of sports. This section explores how "Hoosiers" captures the essence of the state tournament, from the sectional championships to the climactic state finals at the iconic Hinkle Fieldhouse.

Through interviews with basketball historians and those who experienced Indiana's state tournament firsthand, the chapter delves into the traditions, rituals, and fervor that define this annual event. From the thrill of buzzer-beaters to the roar of the crowd, we explore how the film authentically recreates the magic and intensity of the state basketball tournament.

Jimmy Chitwood and the Hoosier Hero: Mythology in Motion

In the realm of Indiana high school basketball, the hero is often an unlikely figure who emerges from the ranks of local talent. Jimmy Chitwood, portrayed by Maris Valainis, embodies this archetype in "Hoosiers." This section explores the mythology of the Hoosier hero and how the character of Jimmy Chitwood becomes a symbol of the unassuming yet extraordinary talent that defines Indiana's basketball narrative.

Through interviews with the cast and basketball analysts, the chapter examines the creation of Jimmy Chitwood's character and how he encapsulates the idea of the Hoosier hero. The section also explores the impact of Chitwood's character on the film's narrative and its resonance with audiences who see in him the embodiment of every small-town dream.

The Victory of the Underdog: Resonance Beyond Indiana

While "Hoosiers" is deeply rooted in the specificity of Indiana's basketball culture, its resonance extends far beyond state borders. This section explores how the film's portrayal of the underdog narrative, the magic of high school hoops, and the symbiotic relationship between the team and the community have universal appeal.

Through interviews with cultural critics and sports movie enthusiasts, the chapter delves into the reasons why "Hoosiers" has become a cultural touchstone for audiences who may not have experienced Indiana's basketball fervor firsthand. From its exploration of human resilience to its celebration of the triumph of the underdog, the film's themes transcend geography and resonate with the broader human experience.

Hoosiers' Legacy: Immortalizing Indiana High School Hoops

As we conclude our exploration of "Capturing the Magic of Indiana High School Hoops," it becomes evident that "Hoosiers" is more than a sports movie; it is a cinematic love letter to the magic of Indiana high school basketball. The chapter invites readers to reflect on how the film immortalizes the cultural and emotional tapestry of Hoosier Hysteria, becoming a timeless testament to the enduring magic of the game at its most grassroots level. Through the lens of "Hoosiers," the enchantment of Indiana high school hoops is not just a local phenomenon; it becomes a universal celebration of community, resilience, and the transformative power of sports.

Cementing Its Place as a Sports Movie Classic

In the pantheon of sports cinema, certain films transcend their genre to become timeless classics that resonate with audiences across generations. "Hoosiers" (1986) is undeniably one of these cinematic gems, a film that has cemented its place as a sports movie classic. This chapter delves into the elements that contribute to the enduring legacy of "Hoosiers," exploring how the film's narrative, characters, and cinematic craftsmanship have solidified its status as an indelible part of the sports movie canon.

The Anatomy of a Classic: Defining Sports Movie Tropes

"Hoosiers" didn't merely follow the playbook of sports movies that came before it; it redefined the rules, creating a narrative template that would influence the genre for years to come. This section explores the defining sports movie tropes that "Hoosiers" both embraced and subverted, examining how the film's adherence to and departure from conventions contributed to its classic status.

Through interviews with film scholars and genre experts, the chapter navigates the tropes such as the underdog narrative, the inspirational coach, and the climactic championship game. It dissects how "Hoosiers" skillfully navigates these tropes, infusing them with a unique authenticity that sets the film apart from its contemporaries.

Character-driven Excellence: The Power of Hickory's Ensemble Cast

At the heart of any classic film is a cast of characters that transcends the screen to become etched in the collective memory of audiences. This section explores how the ensemble cast of "Hoosiers," led by Gene Hackman as Coach Norman Dale, contributes to the film's classic status. Through interviews with the cast, director David Anspaugh, and screenwriter Angelo Pizzo, we unravel the collaborative process that brought these characters to life.

From the stoic leadership of Coach Dale to the endearing quirks of Shooter (Dennis Hopper) and the quiet determination of Jimmy Chitwood (Maris Valainis), the chapter examines how each character becomes a piece of the larger narrative puzzle. The chemistry among the cast, their commitment to authenticity, and the nuanced performances elevate "Hoosiers" beyond a sports drama to a character-driven masterpiece.

Hoosier Authenticity: Cinematic Realism and Basketball Prowess

The authenticity of "Hoosiers" extends beyond the characters to the very fabric of the film itself. This section explores how the commitment to cinematic realism, particularly in its portrayal of basketball, contributes to the film's classic status. Interviews with basketball consultants, players, and the cast provide insights into the rigorous training and choreography that went into capturing the essence of Indiana high school hoops.

The chapter dissects the visual and auditory elements that make the basketball scenes in "Hoosiers" resonate with viewers who appreciate the sport's nuances. From the echoing bounce of the ball in a small-town gym to the strategic plays that unfold on the court, the film's dedication to authenticity becomes a defining feature of its classic appeal.

Cinematic Mastery: The Directorial Vision of David Anspaugh

Behind every classic film is a visionary director who brings the narrative to life with a distinct visual style. This section explores the directorial prowess of David Anspaugh and how his vision shaped the cinematic landscape of "Hoosiers." Through interviews with Anspaugh, cinematographers, and production designers, we delve into the director's creative choices, from the framing of shots to the use of lighting to evoke the intimate feel of small-town Indiana.

The chapter examines Anspaugh's directorial philosophy, his collaboration with the cast, and the challenges of filming on location. It navigates the decisions that contributed to the film's visual appeal and how Anspaugh's directorial acumen elevated "Hoosiers" from a sports drama to a cinematic masterpiece.

Scripting Excellence: Angelo Pizzo's Narrative Alchemy

A classic film often begins with a compelling script, and "Hoosiers" is no exception. This section explores the narrative alchemy of screenwriter Angelo Pizzo, examining how his script became the foundation for the film's enduring legacy. Through interviews with Pizzo, the cast, and Anspaugh, we unravel the creative process that transformed historical events into a timeless narrative.

The chapter navigates Pizzo's approach to storytelling, character development, and the delicate balance between historical accuracy and cinematic storytelling. From crafting memorable dialogue to infusing the script with emotional resonance, Pizzo's narrative prowess becomes a key element in "Hoosiers" securing its place as a sports movie classic.

Critical Acclaim and Audience Reception: The Echo of Applause

A classic film is often defined by the applause it receives from critics and audiences alike. This section explores the critical acclaim and audience reception that accompanied the release of "Hoosiers." Through reviews, interviews with film critics, and retrospectives, the chapter delves into the initial reactions to the film and how it gradually earned its status as a cinematic triumph.

The chapter examines the reasons behind the film's resonance with audiences, including its universal themes, relatable characters, and authentic portrayal of small-town life. It navigates the awards and nominations that followed, illustrating how "Hoosiers" garnered recognition not just as a sports movie but as a classic work of cinema.

Cultural Impact: Beyond the Hardwood

A classic film doesn't merely exist within the confines of its runtime; it extends its influence beyond the screen, shaping cultural conversations and leaving an indelible mark. This section explores the cultural impact of "Hoosiers," examining how the film's themes and characters have become embedded in the broader cultural narrative.

Through interviews with cultural critics, historians, and sports enthusiasts, the chapter unravels the ways in which "Hoosiers" has influenced discussions about sports, small-town life, and the American Dream. From its inclusion in academic curricula to its role in shaping conversations about resilience and community, the film's impact becomes a testament to its classic status.

Legacy of a Classic: Hoosiers' Timeless Resonance

As we conclude our exploration of "Cementing Its Place as a Sports Movie Classic," it becomes evident that "Hoosiers" is not merely a film frozen in time; it is a cinematic classic that continues to resonate with audiences across the years. The chapter invites readers to reflect on how the film's narrative excellence, character-driven storytelling, cinematic authenticity, and cultural impact have collectively woven a legacy that extends far beyond the hardwood. "Hoosiers" is not just a classic sports movie; it is a timeless exploration of the human spirit, community, and the enduring magic of a small-town basketball team that has etched itself into the cultural consciousness as a true cinematic masterpiece.

Chapter 3 - Love & Basketball (2000)
Gina Prince-Bythewood Puts a Fresh Spin on NBA Dreams

In the realm of sports cinema, "Love & Basketball" (2000) emerges as a groundbreaking work that transcends the boundaries of traditional sports narratives. Under the directorial lens of Gina Prince-Bythewood, the film weaves a tale that is as much about love, identity, and aspiration as it is about the game of basketball. This chapter explores how Gina Prince-Bythewood puts a fresh spin on NBA dreams, redefining the genre and opening new avenues for storytelling that resonate with audiences far beyond the hardwood.

Reimagining the Genre: Love, Identity, and the Game

From its opening scenes on a basketball court in 1981 to the climactic moments in the WNBA, "Love & Basketball" is a film that defies genre conventions. This section delves into how Gina Prince-Bythewood reimagines the sports movie genre, infusing it with a narrative that seamlessly blends the personal and the professional, love and ambition.

Through interviews with the director, cast, and film scholars, the chapter navigates the creative decisions that shaped the film's unique identity. From the coming-of-age elements to the exploration of love as a central theme, we unravel how Prince-Bythewood's directorial vision dismantles stereotypes and introduces a fresh perspective to NBA dreams in cinema.

A Love Story Beyond the Court: Monica and Quincy's Journey

At the heart of "Love & Basketball" is a love story that transcends the confines of the basketball court. This section explores how the characters of Monica Wright (Sanaa Lathan) and Quincy McCall (Omar Epps) become the focal points of a narrative that intertwines personal and professional growth. Through interviews with the cast and director, we delve into the character development and the chemistry that defines Monica and Quincy's journey.

The chapter examines the evolution of their relationship, from childhood neighbors shooting hoops to the complexities of adulthood. It explores how Prince-Bythewood portrays love as a dynamic force that intersects with the characters' ambitions, dreams, and individual growth. The film's unique approach to the love story becomes a defining feature that sets it apart in the landscape of sports cinema.

Monica Wright: Breaking Barriers in Basketball Cinema

Monica Wright emerges as a trailblazing character in the world of basketball cinema, challenging stereotypes and breaking new ground. This section explores how Sanaa Lathan's portrayal of Monica contributes to the character's significance and the broader impact on the representation of women in sports movies.

Through interviews with Lathan, Prince-Bythewood, and basketball experts, the chapter delves into the physical and emotional demands of portraying a female athlete. It navigates Monica's journey from a determined young girl challenging societal expectations to a professional basketball player who defies conventions. The section also explores the resonance of

Monica's character with audiences who see in her a representation of unapologetic ambition and resilience.

Quincy McCall: Redefining Masculinity in Sports Cinema

In the realm of sports cinema, male protagonists often adhere to certain archetypes. Quincy McCall, portrayed by Omar Epps, disrupts these conventions, offering a nuanced portrayal of masculinity. This section explores how Quincy's character redefines masculinity in the context of sports movies and how Epps' performance contributes to the character's complexity.

Through interviews with Epps, Prince-Bythewood, and cultural analysts, the chapter navigates Quincy's evolution from a cocky young player to a man grappling with the expectations placed on him. It delves into the vulnerability and emotional depth that Epps brings to the character, challenging traditional notions of what it means to be a male athlete in cinematic narratives.

Gender Dynamics on the Court: A Cinematic Exploration

"Love & Basketball" doesn't merely depict basketball as a backdrop; it uses the court as a stage to explore gender dynamics, equality, and the challenges faced by female athletes. This section examines how the film navigates the complexities of gender in the world of sports, offering a nuanced portrayal that goes beyond the traditional sports movie lens.

Through interviews with the director, cast, and gender studies experts, the chapter dissects key scenes that capture the challenges Monica faces as a female athlete striving for recognition and equality. It also explores how the film challenges stereotypes and invites audiences to question societal expectations placed on women pursuing careers in professional sports.

Soundtrack as Narrative: Musical Beats of Love & Basketball

The film's soundtrack becomes a narrative force of its own, seamlessly integrating with the storytelling to enhance the emotional resonance of the film. This section explores the significance of the soundtrack in "Love & Basketball," examining how the musical choices contribute to the film's unique atmosphere and emotional impact.

Through interviews with the director, music supervisor, and composer, the chapter delves into the process of selecting tracks that complement the narrative beats. It explores how the soundtrack becomes a character in itself, evoking a sense of nostalgia and cultural authenticity. The section also discusses the impact of the film's signature song, "Forever," by Grammy-winning artist and composer Quincy Jones III.

Race and Representation: A Pioneering Perspective

"Love & Basketball" becomes a trailblazer in addressing race and representation within the context of sports cinema. This section explores how the film tackles issues of race and identity, offering a perspective that goes beyond the traditional narratives of the genre. Through interviews with the director, cast, and cultural critics, the chapter delves into the ways in which the film addresses racial dynamics in the world of basketball and society at large.

From the challenges faced by Quincy as a black athlete to Monica's journey in navigating racial and gender expectations, the section examines key scenes that contribute to the film's groundbreaking approach to representation. It also discusses the impact of "Love & Basketball" in opening up conversations about diversity and inclusion in sports movies.

Prince-Bythewood's Directorial Signature: Aesthetic Choices and Visual Storytelling

Gina Prince-Bythewood's directorial signature is imprinted on every frame of "Love & Basketball." This section explores the aesthetic choices and visual storytelling techniques that define the director's approach to NBA dreams and personal narratives. Through interviews with the director, cinematographers, and production designers, the chapter delves into the creative decisions that shape the film's visual identity.

From the use of intimate close-ups to the dynamic cinematography during basketball sequences, the section navigates the director's commitment to visual storytelling that captures both the emotional nuances of the characters and the kinetic energy of the sport. It examines how Prince-Bythewood's directorial choices contribute to the film's unique blend of intimacy and athleticism.

Critical Acclaim and Cultural Impact: Love & Basketball's Enduring Resonance

"Love & Basketball" received widespread critical acclaim upon its release, and its cultural impact has only grown over the years. This section explores the reviews, awards, and retrospectives that highlight the film's significance in both the sports movie genre and broader cultural conversations.

Through interviews with film critics, scholars, and cultural analysts, the chapter navigates the reasons behind the film's critical success and its lasting impact. It examines how "Love & Basketball" has become a cultural touchstone, influencing subsequent films and contributing to discussions about representation, gender dynamics, and the intersection of personal and professional aspirations.

Legacy of Love & Basketball: Paving the Way for New Narratives

As we conclude our exploration of "Gina Prince-Bythewood Puts a Fresh Spin on NBA Dreams," it becomes evident that "Love & Basketball" is more than a sports movie; it is a pioneering work that has left an indelible mark on cinematic storytelling. The chapter invites readers to reflect on how the film's reimagining of NBA dreams, its exploration of love and identity, and its commitment to diverse representation have collectively paved the way for new narratives in sports cinema. "Love & Basketball" stands as a testament to the power of storytelling to challenge conventions, break barriers, and offer fresh perspectives on the universal themes of love, ambition, and the pursuit of dreams.

Omar Epps and Sanaa Lathan's Chemistry Powers the Narrative

In the realm of cinematic storytelling, the magic of a film often resides in the chemistry between its lead actors. "Love & Basketball" elevates this magic to new heights with the undeniable and palpable chemistry between its stars, Omar Epps and Sanaa Lathan. This section explores how Epps and Lathan's on-screen chemistry becomes the beating heart of the narrative, infusing the film with authenticity, emotion, and a timeless quality that resonates with audiences.

Setting the Stage: Monica and Quincy's Journey from Childhood to Adulthood

The narrative tapestry of "Love & Basketball" unfolds across the years, tracing the intertwined lives of Monica Wright and Quincy McCall from childhood to adulthood. This section sets the stage for understanding the arc of Monica and Quincy's relationship, exploring the dynamics of their characters and the pivotal moments that shape their connection.

Through interviews with Omar Epps, Sanaa Lathan, and director Gina Prince-Bythewood, we delve into the actors' initial impressions of their characters and the nuances that attracted them to the roles. The section also explores the challenges and excitement of portraying characters across different life stages, from the innocent days of childhood friendship to the complexities of adult relationships.

From Neighbors to Competitors: Capturing the Essence of Childhood Friendship

The foundation of Monica and Quincy's relationship is laid in their childhood, where they transition from being next-door neighbors to becoming fierce competitors on the basketball court. This section explores how Epps and Lathan capture the essence of childhood friendship, infusing their performances with a sense of innocence, camaraderie, and unspoken understanding.

Through behind-the-scenes anecdotes, interviews, and analysis of key scenes, we unravel the actors' approach to portraying the nuanced dynamics of childhood friendship. The chemistry between Epps and Lathan becomes a driving force, conveying the unbreakable bond between Monica and Quincy and setting the emotional stage for the challenges and growth that lie ahead.

Love on the Court: The Evolution of Monica and Quincy's Relationship

As Monica and Quincy navigate the challenges of adolescence and the competitive world of high school basketball, their relationship takes on new dimensions. This section explores how Epps and Lathan portray the evolving dynamics of love, friendship, and ambition, capturing the emotional complexity of teenage romance.

Through interviews with the actors and director, we dissect key scenes that showcase the characters' growth and the actors' ability to convey the intricacies of teenage emotions. The section also delves into the challenges of filming intimate scenes and the collaborative process between Epps, Lathan, and Prince-Bythewood in crafting a narrative that feels authentic and resonant.

Beyond the Courtship: Adult Challenges and Relationship Realities

The narrative of "Love & Basketball" transcends the typical sports movie romance, venturing into the complexities of adulthood, career aspirations, and the challenges of maintaining a relationship. This section explores how Epps and Lathan navigate the adult phase of Monica and Quincy's journey, portraying characters who grapple with personal ambitions, external pressures, and the realities of love.

Through in-depth interviews with the actors, we delve into their perspectives on portraying adult relationships in the context of a sports movie. The section examines how the chemistry between Epps and Lathan adapts to the changing dynamics of Monica and Quincy's lives, offering a nuanced portrayal of the challenges and compromises that come with growing up and pursuing dreams.

Intimacy and Vulnerability: The Power of Epps and Lathan's Performances

The authenticity of Monica and Quincy's relationship is heightened by the vulnerability and intimacy that Epps and Lathan bring to their performances. This section explores how the actors convey the emotional depth of their characters, from moments of joy and triumph to scenes of heartbreak and resilience.

Through discussions with the actors and director, we unravel the behind-the-scenes process of crafting emotionally charged scenes. The section also examines the actors' approach to portraying vulnerability, the trust built between Epps and Lathan, and the collaborative effort to create a narrative that resonates on a deeply emotional level.

The Basketball Connection: Choreographing Athleticism and Emotion

In a film where basketball is not just a backdrop but a crucial element of the narrative, Epps and Lathan seamlessly blend athleticism with emotion. This section explores how the actors, both known for their physical prowess, bring authenticity to the basketball sequences, creating a seamless connection between the sport and the characters' emotional journeys.

Through interviews with the actors, basketball consultants, and the director, we dissect the training and choreography that went into capturing the intensity and grace of basketball on screen. The section also explores how the athleticism of Epps and Lathan enhances the narrative, making the basketball sequences not just sports action but an integral part of Monica and Quincy's shared passion.

Off-Screen Dynamics: Building a Friendship Beyond the Set

The chemistry between Epps and Lathan isn't confined to the screen; it extends to their off-screen dynamic, creating a genuine friendship that contributes to the authenticity of their performances. This section explores the camaraderie between the actors, their shared experiences during filming, and the lasting impact of their collaboration.

Through interviews with Epps, Lathan, and anecdotes from the set, we gain insights into the actors' friendship, the support they provided for each other, and the shared dedication to bringing Monica and Quincy's story to life. The section also examines how the off-screen rapport between Epps and Lathan enriches the on-screen chemistry, creating a synergy that resonates with audiences.

Audience Reception: The Impact of Epps and Lathan's Chemistry

The magic of Epps and Lathan's chemistry reverberates beyond the set, influencing the way audiences perceive and connect with "Love & Basketball." This section explores the audience reception to the on-screen relationship, examining the impact of Epps and Lathan's performances on viewers' emotional engagement with the narrative.

Through reviews, fan reactions, and cultural analysis, we navigate the ways in which the chemistry between Epps and Lathan contributes to the film's enduring popularity. The section also discusses the actors' interactions with fans and the ways in which audiences have embraced Monica and Quincy's love story as a timeless and resonant cinematic experience.

Legacy of Chemistry: Epps and Lathan's Enduring Impact

As we conclude our exploration of "Omar Epps and Sanaa Lathan's Chemistry Powers the Narrative," it becomes evident that the magic created by Epps and Lathan extends far beyond the frames of "Love & Basketball." The chapter invites readers to reflect on how the actors' chemistry elevates the film from a sports romance to a timeless exploration of love, ambition, and the enduring connections that shape our lives. Epps and Lathan's performances, both individually and as a dynamic duo, contribute to the lasting legacy of "Love & Basketball" as a film that not only redefines sports cinema but also stands as a testament to the transformative power of on-screen chemistry in crafting narratives that resonate across generations.

A Nuanced Perspective on Young Black Love and Aspirations

In the landscape of cinema, the portrayal of love stories has often been tethered to conventional narratives. "Love & Basketball" emerges as a cinematic force that transcends norms, offering a nuanced perspective on young Black love and aspirations. This section delves into how the film, under the directorial vision of Gina Prince-Bythewood, redefines romantic storytelling, exploring the intersection of culture, identity, and personal ambition.

The Tapestry of Young Black Love: Departing from Stereotypes

"Love & Basketball" introduces audiences to a love story that goes beyond clichés and stereotypes. This section examines how the film departs from conventional narratives, offering a fresh perspective on young Black love. Through interviews with Gina Prince-Bythewood, the cast, and cultural critics, we unravel the director's intentional departure from tropes and the impact of presenting a narrative that resonates with authenticity.

The chapter navigates the historical context of Black love in cinema and how "Love & Basketball" becomes a trailblazer in portraying a relationship that is not defined by archaic tropes but is allowed to evolve organically. It explores the nuances of Monica and Quincy's love, free from the burden of racial stereotypes, and the impact of presenting a genuine portrayal of young Black love.

The Cultural Landscape of South Central LA: Setting the Stage

"Love & Basketball" unfolds against the backdrop of South Central Los Angeles, a locale infused with its own cultural tapestry. This section explores how the film utilizes its setting to enrich the narrative, capturing the essence of the community and providing a context for the characters' experiences.

Through discussions with the director, production designers, and cultural historians, the chapter delves into the process of recreating South Central LA in the late '80s and '90s. It examines the cultural elements embedded in the film's visual storytelling, from the music choices to the fashion aesthetics, and how the setting becomes an integral part of the nuanced portrayal of young Black love and aspirations.

Breaking the Mold: Monica Wright as a Complex Protagonist

Monica Wright defies the limitations often imposed on female characters, especially those of color, in romantic narratives. This section explores how Gina Prince-Bythewood and Sanaa Lathan collaborate to create a character who transcends stereotypes, offering a nuanced depiction of a young Black woman navigating love, sports, and personal aspirations.

Through interviews with Sanaa Lathan and the director, we delve into the character development of Monica Wright. The section examines Monica's complexities, from her fierce determination on the basketball court to her vulnerability in matters of the heart. It also explores the impact of presenting a Black female protagonist who is unapologetically ambitious, multi-dimensional, and challenges the expectations placed upon her.

Championing Black Masculinity: Quincy McCall's Journey

In the realm of young Black love, the character of Quincy McCall becomes a pivotal element in the narrative. This section explores how Omar Epps, under the directorial guidance of Prince-Bythewood, brings depth and authenticity to the portrayal of Quincy, challenging stereotypes and presenting a nuanced perspective on Black masculinity.

Through interviews with Omar Epps and the director, the chapter navigates Quincy's journey from a cocky teenage basketball prodigy to a man grappling with the complexities of adulthood. It explores the challenges of portraying a young Black man who defies traditional expectations, the vulnerabilities beneath his exterior, and the impact of showcasing a male character who embraces both ambition and emotional growth.

The Intersectionality of Love and Ambition: Balancing Act

"Love & Basketball" stands as a narrative that explores the delicate balance between personal aspirations and the complexities of love. This section delves into how the film navigates the intersectionality of Monica and Quincy's love story and their individual journeys toward success in the world of basketball.

Through scene analysis and interviews with the director and cast, the chapter dissects key moments that highlight the challenges faced by the protagonists as they pursue their dreams. It explores how the film presents a narrative where love and ambition are not mutually exclusive but are intricately woven into the fabric of the characters' lives.

Friendship, Rivalry, and Love: The Dynamics of Monica and Quincy's Relationship

The foundation of Monica and Quincy's love story is laid in the dynamics of friendship and rivalry. This section explores how the film navigates the complexities of their relationship, from childhood friends to fierce competitors on the court. Through interviews with the actors and director, the chapter delves into the nuances of portraying a relationship that evolves through friendship, competition, and ultimately, love.

It analyzes key scenes that capture the ebb and flow of Monica and Quincy's connection, exploring the chemistry between Sanaa Lathan and Omar Epps that brings authenticity to their interactions. The section also examines how the film challenges traditional romantic narratives by presenting a love story that is built on a foundation of mutual respect, shared passion, and individual growth.

Parental Influence and Cultural Expectations: Family Dynamics

In the exploration of young Black love, "Love & Basketball" introduces the influential role of family dynamics and cultural expectations. This section delves into how the film navigates the impact of parental influence on Monica and Quincy's choices, highlighting the complexities of familial expectations and the pursuit of personal aspirations.

Through interviews with the director, the cast, and cultural analysts, the chapter examines how the characters' relationships with their parents shape their attitudes toward love and ambition. It explores the cultural nuances embedded in the narrative, from Monica's relationship with her strict father to Quincy's complex dynamic with his famous basketball player father.

Authentic Dialogue and Cultural Nuances: Crafting Real Conversations

The authenticity of "Love & Basketball" extends to its dialogue, which captures the cadence and nuances of young Black love. This section explores how Gina Prince-Bythewood, along with the actors, crafts real and relatable conversations that resonate with authenticity.

Through scene analysis and interviews with the director and cast, the chapter delves into the collaborative process of developing dialogue that reflects the cultural and generational context of the characters. It examines the impact of presenting conversations that feel genuine and relatable, contributing to the film's portrayal of young Black love as a rich and nuanced experience.

Soundtrack as a Cultural Soundboard: Music in Love & Basketball

Music becomes an integral part of the cultural narrative in "Love & Basketball," reflecting the emotions and experiences of the characters. This section explores the significance of the film's soundtrack, examining how the music choices contribute to the cultural authenticity of the narrative.

Through interviews with the director, music supervisor, and cultural historians, the chapter delves into the process of selecting tracks that resonate with the themes of love, ambition, and cultural identity. It explores how the soundtrack becomes a cultural soundboard, echoing the emotions of the characters and enriching the film's portrayal of young Black love.

Critical Acclaim and Cultural Impact: Love & Basketball's Enduring Legacy

As we conclude our exploration of "A Nuanced Perspective on Young Black Love and Aspirations," it becomes evident that "Love & Basketball" stands as a cinematic gem that transcends its genre. The chapter invites readers to reflect on how the film's nuanced portrayal of young Black love, its departure from stereotypes, and its exploration of cultural and familial dynamics have collectively contributed to its enduring legacy. "Love & Basketball" not only redefines the landscape of romantic storytelling but also becomes a cultural touchstone, offering a narrative that resonates with authenticity and remains a timeless exploration of love, ambition, and the pursuit of dreams within the context of young Black lives.

The Rare Basketball Movie Led by a Woman's Perspective

In the male-dominated arena of sports cinema, "Love & Basketball" emerges as a trailblazer, not just for its captivating love story but for being a rare basketball movie led by a woman's perspective. This section delves into how director Gina Prince-Bythewood shatters stereotypes, offering a fresh lens on the world of basketball through the eyes of a female protagonist, and how this perspective enriches the film's narrative and cultural impact.

The Landscape of Sports Cinema: Breaking the Mold

Sports movies have historically been a domain dominated by male narratives, both on and off the screen. This section sets the stage by exploring the broader context of sports cinema and the prevailing gender dynamics in the portrayal of athletic stories. Through interviews with Gina Prince-Bythewood and cultural critics, we delve into the challenges faced by female directors in the sports genre and the groundbreaking nature of "Love & Basketball" in breaking the mold.

The chapter navigates the historical representation of women in sports movies, highlighting the scarcity of films that foreground female perspectives in the world of athletics. It explores how "Love & Basketball" becomes a transformative force by placing a woman at the center of a basketball narrative, challenging stereotypes, and expanding the scope of sports cinema.

Directorial Vision: Gina Prince-Bythewood's Impact

Gina Prince-Bythewood's directorial vision becomes a driving force in shaping "Love & Basketball" as more than just a love story set against the backdrop of basketball. This section explores how the director's unique perspective, experiences, and commitment to authenticity contribute to the film's groundbreaking status.

Through interviews with Prince-Bythewood and film scholars, we dissect the director's journey in bringing her vision to life. The section also examines the impact of having a woman behind the camera, from the nuanced portrayal of the female protagonist to the thematic choices that set "Love & Basketball" apart in the realm of sports cinema.

Monica Wright: A Woman in a Man's World

Monica Wright's character, portrayed by Sanaa Lathan, becomes a symbolic figure within the narrative—a woman navigating a traditionally male-dominated space. This section explores how Monica's journey reflects the broader challenges faced by women in pursuing careers in professional sports and how the character's resilience and determination resonate with audiences.

Through interviews with Sanaa Lathan, Gina Prince-Bythewood, and gender studies experts, the chapter delves into the character's creation. It explores Monica's experiences as a female athlete in a highly competitive environment, the scrutiny she faces, and the empowerment derived from challenging gender norms. The section also examines how Monica's journey becomes a metaphor for the broader struggles of women breaking barriers in sports.

Beyond the Locker Room: A Holistic View of Monica's Life

"Love & Basketball" refuses to reduce Monica's character to a one-dimensional athlete. This section explores how the film provides a holistic view of Monica's life, going beyond the locker room to portray her relationships, aspirations, and personal growth. Through scene analysis and interviews with the director and cast, we unravel how the narrative balances Monica's identity as a woman, a friend, a lover, and an athlete.

The chapter also delves into the portrayal of Monica's relationships outside of basketball, including her friendship with Lena (played by Alfre Woodard's real-life daughter, Shareefah), her dynamic with her strict father (Dennis Haysbert), and her romantic entanglements with Quincy. It examines how these elements contribute to a more comprehensive and authentic representation of a woman's life in the world of sports.

Romance and Ambition: Navigating Complexities

"Love & Basketball" seamlessly weaves romance and ambition into its narrative, offering a portrayal of a woman who is not forced to choose between love and her career. This section explores how the film navigates the complexities of Monica's romantic relationship with Quincy while simultaneously pursuing her dreams on the basketball court.

Through interviews with the director, the cast, and relationship experts, the chapter delves into the challenges faced by women in balancing personal relationships with professional aspirations. It explores how Monica becomes a symbol of empowerment, challenging the notion that a woman must compromise her dreams for the sake of love. The section also discusses the impact of presenting a narrative that defies traditional gender norms in the realm of romance and sports.

The Basketball Sequences: Femininity and Athleticism

"Love & Basketball" doesn't shy away from showcasing Monica's athleticism, and this section explores how the basketball sequences are crafted to authentically represent a woman's experience on the court. Through interviews with the director, basketball consultants, and Sanaa Lathan, the chapter delves into the training and choreography that went into capturing the grace, strength, and femininity of Monica's basketball prowess.

The chapter also examines the impact of presenting a female athlete who excels in a sport traditionally associated with men. It explores how the basketball sequences become a celebration of femininity, athleticism, and the breaking of stereotypes, contributing to the film's unique position in sports cinema.

Feminine Aesthetics: Costumes and Styling

The visual representation of Monica extends beyond the basketball court to her everyday life, and this section explores the significance of feminine aesthetics in the film. Through interviews with the costume designer, production designers, and cultural historians, the chapter delves into the choices made in styling Monica's character and the impact of presenting a female protagonist with a distinctive and authentic visual identity.

The section examines Monica's fashion choices, hairstyles, and overall presentation, exploring how these elements contribute to a portrayal that goes beyond sports stereotypes. It also discusses the importance of showcasing a woman who embraces her femininity while excelling in a traditionally male-dominated field.

The Impact of Monica's Story: Opening Doors for Representation

As we explore "The Rare Basketball Movie Led by a Woman's Perspective," it becomes evident that Monica's story extends beyond the screen. The chapter invites readers to reflect on the broader impact of presenting a female protagonist in the world of basketball cinema. Through cultural analysis, interviews with scholars, and audience reactions, the section explores how Monica's character opens doors for increased representation and challenges the industry's traditional gender norms.

The chapter also delves into the ways in which "Love & Basketball" has become a touchstone for female athletes and filmmakers, influencing subsequent narratives in sports cinema. It examines the film's legacy in paving the way for more diverse and authentic portrayals of women in the world of sports, both on and off the screen.

Closing Thoughts: The Lasting Legacy of "Love & Basketball"

As we conclude our exploration of "The Rare Basketball Movie Led by a Woman's Perspective," it becomes clear that "Love & Basketball" is not just a love story but a groundbreaking work that challenges conventions and expands the boundaries of sports cinema. The chapter invites readers to consider the lasting legacy of a film that places a woman's perspective at the forefront, reshaping the narrative landscape and leaving an indelible mark on the intersection of romance, sports, and authentic storytelling.

Chapter 4 - He Got Game (1998)
Spike Lee's Stylistic Take on Basketball Dreams

In the vibrant tapestry of basketball cinema, "He Got Game" stands as a testament to the directorial prowess of Spike Lee. This section delves into how Lee, known for his distinctive style and social commentary, brings a unique and stylistic perspective to the portrayal of basketball dreams in this seminal film. Through a lens of visual storytelling, symbolism, and societal critique, Spike Lee crafts a narrative that transcends the court, exploring the intersection of sports, ambition, and the American dream.

Setting the Stage: Spike Lee's Auteur Touch

Before delving into the intricacies of "He Got Game," it's essential to understand the auteurship of Spike Lee. Known for his bold visual style, social commentary, and unapologetic approach to filmmaking, Lee brings a distinct voice to every project. This section explores Lee's background, his impact on cinema, and how his unique aesthetic sets the stage for the stylistic journey through the world of basketball dreams in "He Got Game."

Through interviews with Spike Lee, film critics, and industry experts, we unravel the director's influences, artistic choices, and commitment to addressing societal issues through his work. The section also examines the evolution of Lee's directorial style leading up to "He Got Game," providing a contextual foundation for understanding the film's visual and narrative innovations.

The Visual Poetry of Basketball: Cinematic Aesthetics

"He Got Game" is a visual symphony that transforms the basketball court into a canvas for cinematic poetry. This section explores how Spike Lee, in collaboration with cinematographer Malik Hassan Sayeed, uses visual aesthetics to elevate the portrayal of basketball dreams. Through scene analysis, interviews with the cinematographer, and discussions with visual arts scholars, we delve into the film's visual language, capturing the grace, intensity, and emotional depth of the sport.

The chapter examines the use of dynamic camera movements, unconventional angles, and vivid color palettes that define the film's visual identity. It explores how the cinematography becomes an integral part of the storytelling, creating a sensory experience that immerses the audience in the world of basketball dreams. The section also delves into the symbolism embedded in the visuals, uncovering layers of meaning that enrich the narrative.

Ball is Life: Symbolism and Metaphor in Hoops

Beyond the game itself, basketball in "He Got Game" becomes a symbol laden with cultural, societal, and personal significance. This section dissects the symbolism of basketball in the film, exploring how Spike Lee uses the sport as a metaphor for larger themes, including ambition, identity, and the pursuit of the American dream.

Through interviews with Spike Lee, cultural critics, and sports analysts, the chapter unravels the layers of meaning associated with the basketball motif. It examines how the basketball becomes a vehicle for expressing the characters' aspirations, conflicts, and societal struggles. The section also delves into the use of basketball as a storytelling device, a cultural touchstone, and a lens through which the characters navigate their individual and collective journeys.

Urban Landscapes: The Intersection of Hoops and Society

"He Got Game" unfolds against the backdrop of urban landscapes, and Spike Lee uses this setting to interweave the narratives of basketball dreams and societal realities. This section explores how the film captures the pulse of city life, juxtaposing the aspirations of young athletes with the challenges of inner-city environments. Through discussions with Spike Lee, urban planners, and cultural historians, the chapter delves into the role of the urban landscape as a character in the film, shaping the characters' experiences and reflecting broader social issues.

The section also examines the use of real locations, the integration of basketball courts into the narrative, and the impact of urban settings on the characters' identities. It explores how Spike Lee's portrayal of the urban environment becomes an integral part of the film's stylistic tapestry, creating a visual dialogue between the characters, their dreams, and the communities they inhabit.

Jake Shuttlesworth: A Father's Ambition in Cinematic Frames

At the heart of "He Got Game" is the complex character of Jake Shuttlesworth, portrayed by Denzel Washington. This section explores how Spike Lee visually constructs the narrative of a father's ambition, moral dilemma, and redemption. Through scene analysis, interviews with Denzel Washington, and discussions with film scholars, we delve into the visual storytelling techniques that bring Jake's character to life.

The chapter examines the use of visual motifs, lighting, and framing to convey Jake's internal struggles and the impact of his choices on his son, Jesus. It explores how Spike Lee uses the visual language of cinema to depict the layers of Jake's character, from his time in prison to his pursuit of redemption through his son's basketball talent. The section also delves into the nuances of Denzel Washington's performance and the collaboration between actor and director in crafting a visually compelling portrayal.

Jesus Shuttlesworth: A Basketball Prodigy's Visual Odyssey

The protagonist of "He Got Game," Jesus Shuttlesworth, portrayed by Ray Allen, undergoes a visual odyssey that mirrors his journey from basketball prodigy to a young man grappling with immense pressure. This section explores how Spike Lee visually navigates Jesus's character arc, using cinematic techniques to convey the weight of expectations, personal struggles, and the pursuit of individual identity.

Through interviews with Ray Allen, Spike Lee, and visual arts experts, the chapter analyzes the visual evolution of Jesus's character. It examines the use of camera work, lighting, and editing to capture the intensity of basketball sequences, the internal conflicts faced by the character, and the emotional nuances of his relationships. The section also delves into the collaboration between director and actor in crafting a visually compelling portrayal of a young athlete at the crossroads of fame, family, and personal choices.

Parallel Journeys: Visual Storytelling of Father and Son

"He Got Game" weaves together the parallel journeys of Jake and Jesus Shuttlesworth, creating a visual narrative that reflects the interplay between their individual ambitions. This section explores how Spike Lee employs visual storytelling techniques to depict the symbiotic relationship between father and son, using cinematic aesthetics to emphasize their similarities, conflicts, and divergent paths.

Through scene analysis, interviews with the director and cast, and discussions with visual storytelling experts, the chapter delves into the use of visual parallels, framing, and editing to connect the journeys of Jake and Jesus. It explores how Spike Lee's stylistic choices enhance the emotional resonance of their narratives, creating a visual tapestry that highlights the complexities of familial relationships, ambition, and the pursuit of dreams.

Soundtrack as Cinematic Palette: Musical Aesthetics in "He Got Game"

In addition to its visual prowess, "He Got Game" distinguishes itself through a compelling soundtrack that becomes an integral part of the film's stylistic identity. This section explores how Spike Lee collaborates with composer Aaron Copland and music supervisor Barry Cole to curate a soundtrack that complements the visual narrative and enhances the emotional impact of the film.

Through interviews with Spike Lee, the composer, and music experts, the chapter delves into the process of selecting and composing music for the film. It explores how the soundtrack becomes a cinematic palette, enhancing the storytelling, creating atmosphere, and contributing to the overall emotional resonance. The section also examines the impact of the film's musical aesthetics on the audience's engagement with the narrative.

Cultural Commentary and Contemporary Relevance

As we conclude our exploration of "Spike Lee's Stylistic Take on Basketball Dreams," it's essential to reflect on the film's cultural commentary and its enduring relevance. The chapter invites readers to consider how Spike Lee's unique visual style, social consciousness, and exploration of basketball dreams transcend the cinematic realm, making "He Got Game" a cultural touchstone. Through cultural analysis, audience reactions, and discussions with cultural commentators, the section explores the film's impact on conversations around sports, ambition, and societal challenges. It also examines how the stylistic choices made by Spike Lee contribute to the film's lasting legacy as a cinematic work that goes beyond entertainment, provoking thought and reflection on the intersection of basketball dreams, identity, and the American experience.

Denzel Washington as a Convict Father, Ray Allen as a Phenom Son

In the landscape of sports cinema, "He Got Game" emerges as a poignant exploration of the father-son dynamic, bringing together the formidable talents of Denzel Washington and NBA star Ray Allen. This section delves into the nuanced portrayals of Jake Shuttlesworth and Jesus Shuttlesworth, examining how Denzel Washington's portrayal of a convict father and Ray Allen's debut performance as a basketball prodigy converge to create a compelling narrative of familial bonds, societal pressures, and the pursuit of basketball dreams.

Cinematic Chemistry: Denzel Washington and Ray Allen

At the heart of "He Got Game" is the dynamic between two powerhouse performers: Denzel Washington and Ray Allen. This section explores the casting choices, the collaborative process between the seasoned actor and the NBA rookie, and the resulting on-screen chemistry that elevates the film. Through interviews with Denzel Washington, Ray Allen, and Spike Lee, we unravel the behind-the-scenes dynamics that contribute to the authenticity and emotional depth of their performances.

The chapter delves into the challenges and opportunities presented by casting an athlete in a leading role, examining how Ray Allen's real-life basketball prowess enriches the portrayal of Jesus Shuttlesworth. It explores the mentorship and collaboration between Denzel Washington and Ray Allen, shedding light on how their respective experiences in acting and basketball converge to create a powerful on-screen father-son relationship.

Jake Shuttlesworth: A Father's Redemption

Denzel Washington's portrayal of Jake Shuttlesworth is a masterclass in character complexity, embodying a convict father seeking redemption through the basketball dreams of his son. This section explores Washington's transformative performance, delving into the layers of Jake's character, his moral struggles, and the journey of redemption that unfolds on screen.

Through scene analysis, interviews with Denzel Washington and Spike Lee, and discussions with film scholars, the chapter examines the evolution of Jake Shuttlesworth. It explores how Washington infuses the character with a mix of vulnerability, regret, and determination, creating a multidimensional portrayal that transcends the typical tropes associated with incarcerated fathers in cinema.

The Prison Narrative: Visualizing Incarceration and Redemption

"He Got Game" introduces audiences to Jake Shuttlesworth within the confines of a prison, a visual backdrop that becomes integral to the character's narrative. This section explores how Spike Lee, in collaboration with Denzel Washington, visualizes the prison experience and leverages it as a powerful metaphor for Jake's journey of redemption.

Through interviews with Spike Lee, the cinematographer, and prison reform advocates, the chapter delves into the visual choices made to depict the prison environment. It analyzes the use of lighting, camera angles, and spatial composition to convey the emotional and psychological impact of incarceration. The section also explores how the prison narrative becomes a lens through which the audience views Jake's character, setting the stage for his complex relationship with his son.

Father-Son Dynamics: Navigating Complexity

"He Got Game" transcends the conventional portrayal of father-son relationships, presenting a nuanced exploration of familial dynamics. This section delves into the complexities of the relationship between Jake and Jesus Shuttlesworth, examining how Denzel Washington and Ray Allen navigate the emotional terrain of a fractured family seeking reconciliation.

Through scene analysis, interviews with the actors, and discussions with family therapists, the chapter explores the emotional nuances of the father-son dynamics. It examines how Washington and Allen convey the layers of love, resentment, and yearning for connection. The section also analyzes key scenes that capture the intricacies of their relationship, from confrontations to moments of vulnerability, highlighting the authenticity that both actors bring to their roles.

Basketball as a Bond: Father and Son on the Court

In "He Got Game," the basketball court becomes the arena where the complexities of the father-son relationship are both heightened and reconciled. This section explores how Spike Lee uses the sport as a metaphor for the emotional interplay between Jake and Jesus Shuttlesworth. Through interviews with the director, basketball consultants, and sports psychologists, the chapter examines the symbolic role of basketball in the film.

The section analyzes key basketball sequences, exploring how the sport becomes a medium for communication, conflict resolution, and emotional release for the characters. It delves into the visual storytelling techniques used to capture the intensity of the on-court moments, the physicality of the game, and the emotional impact on the characters. The chapter also explores the significance of basketball as a bonding mechanism, reflecting the shared history and aspirations of father and son.

Ray Allen's Debut Performance: Transitioning from Court to Screen

"He Got Game" marks the cinematic debut of NBA superstar Ray Allen, stepping into the role of Jesus Shuttlesworth. This section explores Allen's transition from the basketball court to the silver screen, examining the challenges, successes, and impact of his performance. Through interviews with Ray Allen, Denzel Washington, and acting coaches, the chapter delves into the actor's journey and the collaborative process that shaped his portrayal of a young basketball prodigy.

The section also explores how Allen's real-life basketball skills influence the authenticity of his on-court scenes. It examines the actor's approach to capturing the emotional depth of Jesus Shuttlesworth, from the pressures of stardom to the personal conflicts faced by the character. The chapter reflects on the significance of casting a professional athlete in a leading role and the contributions Allen brings to the film's exploration of basketball dreams.

The Phenom's Struggle: Jesus Shuttlesworth's Coming of Age

Ray Allen's performance as Jesus Shuttlesworth goes beyond showcasing basketball prowess; it captures the nuanced coming-of-age journey of a young athlete facing societal pressures and personal dilemmas. This section explores the character development of Jesus, analyzing key scenes that highlight the challenges faced by the phenom on his path to self-discovery.

Through scene analysis, interviews with Ray Allen and Spike Lee, and discussions with sports psychologists, the chapter examines how Allen brings authenticity to the portrayal of a young athlete navigating fame, family expectations, and personal aspirations. It delves into the emotional highs and lows experienced by Jesus, from the intensity of basketball competitions to the internal conflicts that shape his character. The section also explores the broader themes of identity, ambition, and the societal expectations placed on young athletes.

Redemption and Reconciliation: A Father's Journey

As we conclude our exploration of "Denzel Washington as a Convict Father, Ray Allen as a Phenom Son," the chapter reflects on the overarching themes of redemption and reconciliation. It invites readers to consider the transformative journey of Jake Shuttlesworth, examining how his quest for redemption and connection with his son resonates beyond the basketball court. Through cultural analysis, audience reactions, and discussions with film scholars, the section explores the impact of this father-son narrative on the broader conversation around family dynamics, forgiveness, and the pursuit of redemption in the realm of sports cinema.

Examining the Ethics of NCAA Recruiting and Scouting

In the riveting narrative of "He Got Game," Spike Lee ventures beyond the basketball court to scrutinize the ethical complexities of NCAA recruiting and scouting. This section unpacks how the film serves as a compelling lens through which to explore the high-stakes world of college basketball recruitment, shedding light on the moral dilemmas faced by young athletes, their families, and the institutions vying for their talents.

The Allure of College Basketball: A Path to Dreams

The chapter kicks off by contextualizing the allure of college basketball, examining its role as a pathway to professional success and a dream realized for many aspiring players. Through interviews with sports historians, former players, and NCAA officials, the section delves into the historical significance of college basketball as a stepping stone for athletes seeking to make their mark on the national stage.

By exploring the unique dynamics of college basketball, the section establishes the backdrop against which the ethical dimensions of NCAA recruiting and scouting unfold in "He Got Game." It considers the cultural and societal significance attached to college basketball, positioning it as a space where dreams are nurtured, and where the ethical boundaries of talent acquisition are tested.

Jesus Shuttlesworth: A Pawn in the Recruiting Game

The narrative arc of "He Got Game" places Jesus Shuttlesworth, a prodigious high school basketball talent, at the center of a high-stakes recruiting battle. This section examines how Jesus becomes a symbolic figure representing the hopes and aspirations of young athletes, while also becoming a pawn in the larger game of NCAA recruitment. Through scene analysis and interviews with Ray Allen, Spike Lee, and sports analysts, the chapter explores the ethical dimensions of recruiting a player of Jesus's caliber.

The section scrutinizes the tactics employed by college recruiters and scouts as they vie for Jesus's commitment. It delves into the moral dilemmas faced by the character as he navigates the pressures of making a life-altering decision. The chapter also analyzes key scenes that depict the intersection of athletic talent, institutional interest, and the personal aspirations of a young athlete.

Fatherly Guidance or Exploitation: Jake's Dilemma

The ethical considerations of NCAA recruiting are further complicated by the involvement of Jake Shuttlesworth, Jesus's father, who is serving time in prison. This section explores the moral dilemma faced by Jake as he grapples with the opportunity presented by college recruiters to secure his son's commitment. Through scene analysis and interviews with Denzel Washington and Spike Lee, the chapter delves into Jake's internal conflict between prioritizing his son's well-being and navigating the ethical gray areas of the recruitment process.

The section examines how the film portrays the exploitation of family circumstances in the pursuit of securing a player's commitment. It considers the power dynamics at play when college recruiters leverage personal situations to gain a competitive edge. The chapter invites readers to reflect on the ethical implications of recruiting decisions that extend beyond the basketball court and delve into the lives and vulnerabilities of young athletes and their families.

Coaches and Compromise: The Institutional Pressure

"He Got Game" sheds light on the pressures faced by college coaches as they navigate the ethical terrain of recruiting. This section explores the institutional dynamics that push coaches to make compromises in their pursuit of top-tier talent. Through interviews with sports ethicists, former coaches, and cultural critics, the chapter delves into the ethical dilemmas faced by those responsible for assembling competitive rosters.

The section analyzes how the film portrays the intense competition among college programs and the lengths to which coaches are willing to go to secure commitments. It examines the ethical considerations of offering scholarships, promises of success, and the potential for professional advancement in exchange for a player's commitment. The chapter also reflects on the broader implications of institutional pressures in college sports and the impact on the ethical compass of those involved.

Legal and Illegal Tactics: Navigating the Gray Areas

"He Got Game" highlights the fine line between legal and illegal tactics employed in the recruitment process. This section dissects the various strategies used by college recruiters, some within the bounds of NCAA regulations and others pushing the ethical boundaries. Through interviews with sports lawyers, NCAA compliance officers, and sports journalists, the chapter examines the legal and ethical considerations at play in the pursuit of top-tier talent.

The section explores how the film portrays the recruitment process as a landscape fraught with gray areas, where the line between ethical and unethical behavior becomes blurred. It analyzes the consequences of legal but ethically questionable tactics, such as promises of future success, inducements, and the exploitation of personal circumstances. The chapter invites readers to reflect on the broader implications for the ethical landscape of college sports and the ongoing debate surrounding NCAA regulations.

Family Pressures and Financial Considerations

"He Got Game" delves into the external pressures faced by young athletes and their families during the recruitment process. This section explores the ethical dimensions of familial expectations, financial considerations, and the potential exploitation of athletes for economic gain. Through interviews with sports psychologists, former athletes, and financial analysts, the chapter examines the impact of family dynamics on the decision-making process.

The section delves into the portrayal of familial pressures faced by Jesus Shuttlesworth, showcasing the ethical dilemmas arising from financial need and the potential for future professional success. It analyzes the ethical considerations of athletes as they navigate the expectations of family members, weighing the promises of financial stability against the potential pitfalls of an uncertain future. The chapter also reflects on the broader societal context that perpetuates these pressures within the framework of college athletics.

The Dark Side of Recruitment: Exploitation and Corruption

"He Got Game" doesn't shy away from exposing the darker side of NCAA recruitment, including instances of exploitation and corruption. This section explores the portrayal of unscrupulous practices, illegal inducements, and the exploitation of young athletes for financial gain. Through interviews with sports journalists, NCAA investigators, and cultural critics, the chapter delves into the film's critique of the corrupt underbelly of college basketball recruitment.

The section analyzes key scenes that shed light on the shadowy dealings within the recruitment process, showcasing the potential for exploitation and the erosion of ethical standards. It invites readers to reflect on the real-world implications of corruption in college sports, considering the impact on the lives of young athletes, the integrity of institutions, and the broader ethical framework of collegiate athletics.

Player Agency and Informed Decision-Making

As we conclude our exploration of "Examining the Ethics of NCAA Recruiting and Scouting," the chapter reflects on the importance of player agency and informed decision-making. It considers how the film prompts a critical examination of the ethical considerations surrounding NCAA recruitment and encourages a discourse on the empowerment of young athletes to make informed choices. Through cultural analysis, audience reactions, and discussions with sports ethicists, the section explores the potential for reform within the recruiting landscape, emphasizing the ethical responsibility of institutions, coaches, and athletes in shaping the future of college sports.

Lee's Signature Flair in Service of a Basketball Story

Spike Lee, a filmmaker renowned for his distinct visual style and social commentary, brings his signature flair to the world of basketball in "He Got Game." This section delves into the artistic choices, narrative techniques, and thematic elements that define Lee's directorial approach, exploring how his unique vision elevates the storytelling and enriches the cinematic portrayal of basketball dreams.

Visual Panache: The Aesthetic Language of Spike Lee

Spike Lee's films are instantly recognizable for their visual panache, and "He Got Game" is no exception. This section delves into Lee's aesthetic choices, examining the use of dynamic camera movements, unconventional angles, and vivid color palettes that define the film's visual identity. Through scene analysis, interviews with the cinematographer, and discussions with visual arts scholars, the chapter explores how Lee's visual language transforms the basketball court into a canvas for cinematic poetry.

The section also considers the influence of Lee's background in fine arts on his approach to cinematography, highlighting how he infuses each frame with deliberate composition and visual symbolism. It examines the director's penchant for kinetic visuals, exploring how his dynamic camera work captures the intensity, athleticism, and emotional depth of basketball sequences. By analyzing key scenes, the chapter unveils the visual motifs that distinguish Lee's directorial style and contribute to the film's overall impact.

Narrative Innovation: Weaving Stories Beyond the Court

Beyond its portrayal of basketball, "He Got Game" weaves a narrative that transcends the confines of the court. This section explores how Spike Lee innovatively intertwines personal narratives, societal commentary, and thematic depth within the framework of a basketball story. Through interviews with the screenwriter, cultural critics, and narrative experts, the chapter analyzes how Lee uses storytelling techniques to create a multi-layered and resonant cinematic experience.

The section delves into the non-linear narrative structure employed by Lee, examining how flashbacks, dream sequences, and parallel storylines contribute to the film's thematic richness. It explores the director's use of intertextuality, incorporating references to literature, music, and popular culture, to enhance the narrative depth. The chapter also considers how Lee's narrative innovation extends the film's impact beyond the sports genre, creating a work that invites audiences to engage with universal themes of family, identity, and the pursuit of dreams.

Character Depth: Humanizing the Athlete

"He Got Game" stands out for its nuanced characterizations, particularly in its portrayal of Jesus Shuttlesworth. This section examines how Spike Lee, known for his emphasis on character depth, humanizes the athlete by delving into the personal struggles, aspirations, and vulnerabilities that define him. Through scene analysis, interviews with the actors, and discussions with character development experts, the chapter explores Lee's commitment to crafting multidimensional characters within the realm of sports cinema.

The section delves into how Lee's directorial approach prioritizes character over caricature, resisting the temptation to reduce athletes to one-dimensional stereotypes. It analyzes key moments that reveal the complexities of Jesus Shuttlesworth, exploring his relationships, internal conflicts, and emotional journey. By humanizing the athlete, Lee challenges traditional sports movie tropes, providing audiences with a more authentic and relatable portrayal of a young man navigating the pressures of fame and familial expectations.

Social Commentary: Basketball as a Microcosm of Society

Spike Lee has long been known for embedding social commentary within his films, and "He Got Game" is a testament to this tradition. This section explores how Lee uses the basketball narrative as a microcosm of societal issues, addressing themes such as race, class, and the American dream. Through interviews with cultural critics, sociologists, and the director himself, the chapter analyzes the layers of social commentary woven into the fabric of the film.

The section delves into the exploration of racial dynamics, examining how the film portrays the challenges faced by black athletes within the context of college recruitment and professional aspirations. It also considers the commentary on economic disparities, showcasing the contrasting realities of inner-city life and the allure of success through basketball. By examining key scenes and symbolic elements, the chapter illuminates how Lee leverages the basketball story to provoke thought and discussion on broader societal issues.

Soundtrack as Narrative Companion: Musical Aesthetics in "He Got Game"

In addition to its visual and narrative dimensions, "He Got Game" distinguishes itself through a compelling soundtrack that becomes an integral part of the storytelling. This section explores how Spike Lee collaborates with composer Aaron Copland and music supervisor Barry Cole to curate a soundtrack that complements the visual narrative and enhances the emotional impact of the film. Through interviews with the director, the composer, and music experts, the chapter delves into the process of selecting and composing music for the film.

The section explores how the soundtrack becomes a narrative companion, shaping the emotional tone of key scenes, creating atmosphere, and reinforcing thematic elements. It considers the integration of diverse musical genres, from hip-hop to orchestral compositions, and how the soundtrack becomes a sonic reflection of the film's multifaceted storytelling. By analyzing the impact of musical aesthetics on the audience's engagement with the narrative, the chapter unveils the symbiotic relationship between sound and image in Lee's directorial flair.

Symbolism and Imagery: Metaphors Beyond the Court

"He Got Game" is rife with symbolism and imagery that extends beyond the basketball court, contributing to the film's thematic depth. This section delves into how Spike Lee utilizes visual metaphors, recurring symbols, and allegorical elements to enrich the cinematic experience. Through scene analysis, interviews with the director, and discussions with visual arts scholars, the chapter explores the layers of meaning embedded in the film's symbolism.

The section examines recurring motifs such as the prison imagery, the Jesus Shuttleworth basketball shoes, and the use of color symbolism to convey thematic messages. It considers how these visual elements become narrative devices, enhancing the storytelling and inviting audiences to engage with the film on multiple levels. By decoding the symbolism and imagery present in "He Got Game," the chapter unveils the intricacies of Lee's directorial craftsmanship and its contribution to the film's enduring impact.

Cinematic Homage: Referencing Basketball History and Culture

Spike Lee, a passionate basketball fan, infuses "He Got Game" with references to the sport's history, culture, and iconic figures. This section explores how Lee pays homage to basketball legends, historical moments, and cultural touchstones, creating a tapestry of cinematic references within the film. Through interviews with the director, basketball historians, and cultural critics, the chapter examines the cinematic homage present in "He Got Game."

The section delves into how Lee integrates archival footage, visual cues, and narrative references to celebrate the legacy of basketball. It explores the inclusion of real-life basketball figures and the portrayal of fictional characters inspired by the sport's rich history. By appreciating the cinematic homage within the film, the chapter offers readers insights into how Spike Lee's passion for basketball becomes a driving force in shaping the narrative, connecting audiences to the cultural tapestry of the sport.

Critical Reception: Lee's Artistic Impact on Sports Cinema

"He Got Game" sparked critical acclaim for Spike Lee's artistic vision and its impact on the sports cinema landscape. This section explores the critical reception of the film, analyzing reviews, awards, and scholarly perspectives that celebrate Lee's contribution to the genre. Through interviews with film critics, scholars, and the director himself, the chapter reflects on how "He Got Game" has left an indelible mark on the intersection of basketball and cinema.

The section examines how critics and scholars have interpreted Lee's directorial choices, praised the film's thematic depth, and celebrated its cultural resonance. It also considers the film's enduring legacy within the broader context of sports cinema, assessing its influence on subsequent basketball-themed films and its place in the canon of Spike Lee's directorial achievements. By unpacking the critical reception, the chapter offers readers a comprehensive understanding of the artistic impact of "He Got Game" on the cinematic portrayal of basketball dreams.

Conclusion: Lee's Ongoing Contribution to Sports Cinema

As we conclude our exploration of "Lee's Signature Flair in Service of a Basketball Story," the chapter reflects on Spike Lee's ongoing contribution to sports cinema. It considers how "He Got Game" stands as a testament to the director's ability to infuse the world of basketball with artistic innovation, social commentary, and a unique cinematic language. Through cultural analysis, audience reactions, and discussions with film scholars, the section offers readers a final appreciation of Spike Lee's enduring impact on the cinematic portrayal of basketball dreams, reinforcing his position as a trailblazer in the intersection of sports and storytelling.

Chapter 5 - White Men Can't Jump (1992)
An Irreverent Buddy Comedy Set in LA Pickup Games

"White Men Can't Jump" leaps onto the basketball film scene with irreverent charm and street-smart humor. Directed by Ron Shelton, the film explores the dynamics of friendship, the clash of stereotypes, and the unique subculture of pickup basketball games in Los Angeles. This section delves into the vibrant world crafted by Shelton, examining how the film navigates the playground courts of LA to deliver a memorable and comedic take on the game.

The Playground as Stage: Setting the Scene

"White Men Can't Jump" introduces audiences to the vibrant and often raucous world of pickup basketball on the playground courts of Los Angeles. This section explores how Ron Shelton uses the playground setting as a dynamic stage for the film's narrative. Through scene analysis, interviews with the director, and discussions with sports historians, the chapter unveils the significance of the playground as a backdrop to the characters' interactions and the overarching themes of the film.

The section delves into the cultural and social aspects of playground basketball, considering how it serves as a microcosm of street culture, athletic prowess, and the clash of diverse personalities. It also examines the visual and auditory elements that characterize the playground scenes, from the vibrant graffiti-covered courts to the rhythmic sound of dribbling basketballs, enhancing the film's authenticity and immersing audiences in the world of pickup games.

Billy Hoyle and Sidney Deane: An Unlikely Duo

At the heart of "White Men Can't Jump" is the dynamic between Billy Hoyle, played by Woody Harrelson, and Sidney Deane, portrayed by Wesley Snipes. This section delves into the unconventional pairing of the two characters, exploring the comedic and dramatic elements that define their on-screen chemistry. Through scene analysis, interviews with the actors, and discussions with the director, the chapter examines how the film subverts stereotypes and explores the complexities of friendship within the context of pickup basketball.

The section explores the character dynamics of Billy and Sidney, considering how their contrasting backgrounds, playing styles, and personalities contribute to the film's humor and narrative depth. It delves into the character development, examining how the film challenges racial and cultural stereotypes by presenting an unlikely alliance between a white player and a black player in a sport often marked by racial divisions. By analyzing key scenes, the chapter unveils the layers of camaraderie, competition, and mutual respect that define the duo's relationship.

Street Smarts and Trash Talk: The Language of Pickup Basketball

"White Men Can't Jump" captures the essence of pickup basketball not only through its visuals but also through the language spoken on the court. This section explores the unique vernacular of pickup games, examining the art of trash talk, the rhythm of on-court communication, and the unwritten rules that govern street basketball. Through interviews with basketball players, linguistic experts, and the director, the chapter delves into how the film authentically captures the linguistic nuances of pickup basketball culture.

The section considers how trash talk becomes a form of self-expression, a strategy to psych out opponents, and a means of asserting dominance on the court. It also explores how the film navigates the delicate balance between competitive banter and potential conflicts, showcasing the verbal jousting that characterizes pickup games. By analyzing key scenes featuring street smarts and trash talk, the chapter unveils the role of language in shaping the on-court experience and contributing to the film's comedic and authentic portrayal of the basketball subculture.

Hoyle's Conundrum: Navigating Stereotypes and Expectations

"White Men Can't Jump" confronts the racial and cultural stereotypes ingrained in the perception of basketball players. This section explores how Billy Hoyle, a white player, grapples with societal expectations and challenges the assumptions associated with his race on the basketball court. Through scene analysis, interviews with the actor, and discussions with cultural critics, the chapter examines how the film uses Hoyle's character arc to subvert stereotypes and provide commentary on race in sports.

The section delves into the challenges faced by Hoyle as he navigates the predominantly black world of pickup basketball. It considers how the film tackles issues of racial prejudice, cultural appropriation, and the expectations placed on individuals based on their race. The chapter also explores the comedic and dramatic dimensions of Hoyle's conundrum, examining how the character's journey becomes a vehicle for social commentary and a critique of the assumptions ingrained in basketball culture.

Sidney's Street Wisdom: Navigating the Playground Subculture

Wesley Snipes' portrayal of Sidney Deane brings to life a character steeped in the streetwise culture of pickup basketball. This section explores how Sidney serves as a guide to the intricacies of the playground subculture, from the unspoken rules to the art of survival on the court. Through scene analysis, interviews with the actor, and discussions with basketball historians, the chapter examines Sidney's role as a mentor and mediator within the world of pickup games.

The section delves into Sidney's street wisdom, considering how the character navigates the complex dynamics of the playground, from negotiating game outcomes to managing interpersonal conflicts. It explores the significance of Sidney's role in contextualizing the cultural nuances of pickup basketball, serving as a bridge between the characters and the audience. By analyzing key scenes featuring Sidney's street smarts, the chapter unveils how the film uses his character to provide insights into the unspoken codes that govern playground basketball.

Love and Basketball: Navigating Relationships Beyond the Court

"White Men Can't Jump" weaves elements of romance into its narrative, exploring the complexities of relationships within the context of pickup basketball. This section delves into the film's portrayal of love and basketball, examining how it intertwines the personal lives of the characters with their on-court dynamics. Through scene analysis, interviews with the director, and discussions with relationship experts, the chapter explores the romantic subplot as a thematic element that adds depth to the film's narrative.

The section considers the relationship between Billy Hoyle and his girlfriend Gloria, played by Rosie Perez, as a lens through which the film explores themes of trust, ambition, and personal growth. It examines how the romantic subplot intersects with the overarching narrative of friendship and competition, providing a nuanced portrayal of the characters' lives beyond the basketball court. By analyzing key scenes that depict the intersection of love and basketball, the chapter unveils the film's ability to balance humor, drama, and romance within the backdrop of pickup games.

Basketball Hustles: From Courtside to Sidelines

"White Men Can't Jump" introduces audiences to the world of basketball hustles, where street smarts and strategic maneuvers extend beyond the court. This section explores how the film portrays the characters' engagement in various basketball-related hustles, from betting on games to participating in street competitions. Through scene analysis, interviews with the director, and discussions with sports historians, the chapter examines the role of basketball hustles as a narrative device that adds layers of intrigue to the film.

The section delves into how the characters navigate the sidelines of pickup basketball, engaging in hustles that range from comical to high-stakes. It considers the impact of hustles on the characters' relationships, motivations, and personal growth. The chapter also explores the film's commentary on the culture of gambling and one-upmanship within the basketball subculture. By analyzing key scenes featuring basketball hustles, the chapter unveils the film's exploration of the characters' resourcefulness and the dynamics that unfold beyond the bounds of the playground.

Beyond the Scoreboard: The Philosophy of Pickup Basketball

"White Men Can't Jump" transcends the traditional sports movie formula by delving into the philosophy of pickup basketball. This section explores how the film goes beyond the scoreboard, using the game as a metaphor for life's challenges and opportunities. Through interviews with the director, basketball philosophers, and discussions with cultural critics, the chapter examines the thematic depth of the film, considering how it uses basketball as a vehicle for philosophical reflections.

The section delves into the film's exploration of themes such as resilience, adaptability, and the pursuit of personal excellence within the context of pickup basketball. It considers how the characters' experiences on the court become metaphors for broader life lessons, illustrating the transformative power of the game. By analyzing key scenes that encapsulate the film's philosophical underpinnings, the chapter unveils the depth of "White Men Can't Jump" as a sports movie that transcends genre conventions, inviting audiences to reflect on the universal aspects of the human experience embedded in the game of basketball.

Cinematic Aesthetics: The Visual Style of Pickup Basketball

Ron Shelton's directorial approach in "White Men Can't Jump" extends beyond narrative and character dynamics to encompass the film's visual aesthetics. This section explores how Shelton uses cinematography, editing, and visual motifs to capture the energy, rhythm, and spontaneity of pickup basketball. Through scene analysis, interviews with the cinematographer, and discussions with visual arts scholars, the chapter examines the film's visual style as a crucial element in conveying the essence of the game.

The section delves into the use of handheld cameras, dynamic tracking shots, and innovative editing techniques that infuse the basketball sequences with a sense of immediacy and authenticity. It considers the visual motifs that define the film's aesthetic language, from slow-motion captures of on-court action to close-ups that reveal the emotional nuances of the characters. By analyzing key visual elements, the chapter unveils how the film's cinematic aesthetics contribute to its immersive portrayal of pickup basketball, enhancing the overall viewing experience.

Critical Reception: The Impact of Irreverent Humor and Streetwise Charm

"White Men Can't Jump" garnered attention not only for its unique take on pickup basketball culture but also for its irreverent humor and streetwise charm. This section explores the critical reception of the film, considering reviews, audience reactions, and scholarly perspectives on its impact. Through interviews with film critics, cultural analysts, and the director, the chapter reflects on how "White Men Can't Jump" has left a lasting imprint on the sports movie genre.

The section examines how critics and audiences responded to the film's blend of comedy, drama, and social commentary. It considers the cultural resonance of the film's exploration of race, friendship, and the dynamics of pickup basketball. The chapter also reflects on the enduring popularity of "White Men Can't Jump" within the broader landscape of sports cinema, assessing its influence on subsequent films and its place in the canon of basketball-themed movies. By unpacking the critical reception, the chapter offers readers insights into the film's cultural impact and the enduring appeal of its irreverent humor and streetwise charm.

Conclusion: The Playground Legacy of "White Men Can't Jump"

As we conclude our exploration of "An Irreverent Buddy Comedy Set in LA Pickup Games," the chapter reflects on the enduring legacy of "White Men Can't Jump" in the realm of basketball cinema. It considers how the film's irreverent humor, streetwise charm, and unique take on pickup basketball culture have solidified its place as a beloved classic. Through cultural analysis, audience reactions, and discussions with film scholars, the section offers readers a final appreciation of the film's impact on the intersection of sports and storytelling, celebrating its contribution to the rich tapestry of basketball-themed movies.

Wesley Snipes and Woody Harrelson's Unlikely Bond

"White Men Can't Jump" stands as a testament to the power of chemistry on screen, particularly in the dynamic pairing of Wesley Snipes and Woody Harrelson. In this section, we explore the unlikely bond forged between these two actors and the magic they brought to the film. Through scene analysis, interviews with the actors, and discussions with the director, we unravel the nuances of their performances and how their camaraderie became the beating heart of this irreverent buddy comedy set in the vibrant world of LA pickup games.

The Casting Alchemy: Bringing Sidney and Billy to Life

The foundation of the film's success lies in the impeccable casting of Wesley Snipes as Sidney Deane and Woody Harrelson as Billy Hoyle. This section explores the casting process, considering how the filmmakers identified and selected Snipes and Harrelson for these iconic roles. Through interviews with the casting director, the director Ron Shelton, and the actors themselves, we delve into the alchemy that brought these characters to life and the unique qualities each actor brought to the table.

The section explores how Snipes and Harrelson, each known for their distinct styles and talents, were cast against type to play characters that defied conventional stereotypes. It examines the director's vision in assembling this unconventional duo and the initial reactions to the casting choices. By analyzing key scenes that showcase the actors' early interactions on screen, the chapter sets the stage for the exploration of their on-screen chemistry and the evolution of an unlikely bond.

On-Screen Dynamics: The Chemistry of Sidney and Billy

The heart of "White Men Can't Jump" lies in the electric chemistry between Wesley Snipes and Woody Harrelson. This section delves into the on-screen dynamics of Sidney and Billy, exploring how Snipes and Harrelson brought these characters to life with authenticity, humor, and a touch of streetwise charm. Through scene analysis, interviews with the actors, and discussions with the director, the chapter examines the nuances of their performances and the evolution of their on-screen bond.

The section considers the initial clash of personalities between Sidney and Billy, highlighting the characters' differences in background, playing style, and street smarts. It explores how the film navigates the tension between them, using humor and witty banter to establish their on-screen dynamic. The chapter also analyzes key scenes that showcase the characters' interactions, from their first pickup game together to the development of a genuine camaraderie. By unraveling the layers of their on-screen dynamics, the section provides insights into the actors' ability to capture the essence of friendship within the context of pickup basketball.

The Subversion of Stereotypes: Sidney and Billy as Iconoclasts

"White Men Can't Jump" subverts stereotypes not only within the narrative but also through the characters of Sidney and Billy. This section explores how Snipes and Harrelson embrace and challenge stereotypes associated with race and athleticism, creating characters that defy expectations. Through interviews with the actors, discussions with cultural critics, and insights from the director, the chapter delves into the iconoclastic nature of Sidney and Billy and the impact of their characterizations on the film's cultural commentary.

The section considers how Sidney challenges traditional stereotypes associated with black athletes, presenting a character who is both street-smart and intellectually savvy. It also explores Billy's character as a white player navigating a predominantly black world, challenging the notion that "white men can't jump." By analyzing scenes that showcase the characters' confrontations with stereotypes, the chapter unveils how Snipes and Harrelson contribute to the film's broader message of breaking free from societal expectations within the realm of pickup basketball.

Banter, Trash Talk, and Verbal Jousting: The Language of Friendship

Friendships on the court are often defined by banter, trash talk, and a unique language of their own. This section explores how Sidney and Billy's friendship is expressed through the witty banter and verbal jousting that characterize their on-screen interactions. Through scene analysis, interviews with the actors, and discussions with linguistic experts, the chapter examines the linguistic nuances of their friendship and how language becomes a vehicle for humor, camaraderie, and the expression of mutual respect.

The section considers the role of trash talk in pickup basketball culture and how it serves as a form of communication and camaraderie between players. It explores the unique verbal dynamics between Sidney and Billy, highlighting how their banter goes beyond the surface to reveal the deeper layers of their friendship. By analyzing key scenes that showcase their verbal exchanges, the chapter unveils how Snipes and Harrelson masterfully navigate the language of friendship, adding authenticity and humor to their on-screen bond.

Navigating the Playground Subculture: Sidney and Billy's Street Smarts

In the playground subculture of pickup basketball, street smarts often matter as much as athletic prowess. This section explores how Sidney and Billy navigate the intricacies of the playground, showcasing their street smarts and survival instincts. Through scene analysis, interviews with the actors, and discussions with sports historians, the chapter examines the characters' ability to read the playground's unspoken rules and adapt to its dynamic subculture.

The section delves into how Sidney's street wisdom becomes a guiding force for Billy as they navigate the challenges of pickup games. It explores the characters' interactions with other players, the nuances of their on-court strategies, and the unspoken codes that govern the playground. By analyzing scenes that depict Sidney and Billy's street smarts, the chapter unveils how Snipes and Harrelson infuse their performances with authenticity, capturing the essence of the playground subculture within the narrative.

The Evolution of Friendship: From Rivals to Allies

"White Men Can't Jump" takes audiences on a journey from rivalry to friendship, as Sidney and Billy evolve from adversaries to allies on the basketball court. This section explores the character development and narrative arc that define the evolution of their friendship. Through scene analysis, interviews with the actors, and discussions with the director, the chapter examines the pivotal moments that shape the characters' relationship and the authenticity Snipes and Harrelson bring to this transformative journey.

The section considers the initial rivalry between Sidney and Billy, fueled by preconceived notions and the competitive nature of pickup basketball. It explores the turning points that lead to their collaboration and the emergence of a genuine bond. The chapter also analyzes key scenes that showcase the characters' growth, from learning to trust each other on the court to forming an enduring friendship. By unraveling the evolution of Sidney and Billy's relationship, the section offers readers insights into how Snipes and Harrelson capture the authenticity and emotional depth of their characters' journey.

Comic Timing and Improvisation: Snipes and Harrelson's Performative Chemistry

Beyond scripted scenes, the magic of Sidney and Billy's friendship comes alive through the actors' comic timing and improvisational skills. This section explores how Wesley Snipes and Woody Harrelson bring spontaneity and humor to their performances, elevating the film's comedic elements. Through interviews with the actors, discussions with the director, and insights from comedy experts, the chapter examines the performative chemistry that contributes to the film's irreverent and entertaining atmosphere.

The section considers the actors' approach to improvisation, exploring how they infused their characters with spontaneity and unexpected comedic moments. It delves into key scenes that highlight Snipes and Harrelson's ability to play off each other's energy, enhancing the humor and authenticity of their on-screen interactions. By unpacking the nuances of their performative chemistry, the chapter provides readers with a deeper appreciation for the comedic prowess that defines Sidney and Billy's dynamic.

Critical Acclaim: Sidney and Billy's Impact on Audience Reception

The success of "White Men Can't Jump" is not only measured by box office numbers but also by the audience's reception and critical acclaim. This section explores how Sidney and Billy's on-screen chemistry contributed to the film's positive reception and enduring popularity. Through reviews, audience reactions, and insights from film critics, the chapter reflects on the impact of Snipes and Harrelson's performances on the overall success of the film.

The section examines how critics and audiences responded to the authenticity and humor brought to Sidney and Billy's friendship. It considers the cultural resonance of their dynamic within the broader context of sports cinema. The chapter also reflects on the enduring appeal of "White Men Can't Jump" and the impact of Snipes and Harrelson's performances on the film's legacy. By unpacking critical acclaim and audience reception, the section offers readers a comprehensive understanding of how Sidney and Billy's on-screen bond contributed to the film's enduring status as a classic.

Conclusion: The Lasting Legacy of Sidney and Billy's Friendship

As we conclude our exploration of "Wesley Snipes and Woody Harrelson's Unlikely Bond," the chapter reflects on the enduring legacy of Sidney and Billy's friendship in the realm of basketball cinema. It considers how Snipes and Harrelson's performances, infused with authenticity, humor, and a touch of streetwise charm, have left an indelible mark on the film's cultural impact. Through cultural analysis, audience reactions, and discussions with film scholars, the section offers readers a final appreciation of the actors' contribution to the rich tapestry of basketball-themed movies, celebrating the lasting legacy of Sidney and Billy's unlikely but unforgettable bond.

Exploring Racial and Class Stereotypes with Humor

"White Men Can't Jump" boldly ventures into the realm of racial and class stereotypes, turning them on their head with a masterful touch of humor. In this section, we delve into how the film navigates these sensitive themes, using wit, satire, and authenticity to challenge preconceptions. Through scene analysis, interviews with the actors, and discussions with cultural critics, we unravel the film's nuanced approach to addressing racial and class stereotypes within the context of the LA pickup basketball scene.

Setting the Scene: LA Playground Culture as a Microcosm

The playgrounds of Los Angeles serve as a microcosm for exploring racial and class dynamics in "White Men Can't Jump." This section examines how the film establishes the playground as a vibrant stage where stereotypes are confronted and subverted. Through scene analysis, interviews with the director, and discussions with sports historians, we explore the cultural and social nuances of the LA playground culture depicted in the film.

The section delves into the visual and auditory elements that characterize the playground scenes, creating an authentic backdrop for the exploration of stereotypes. It considers how the film portrays the diversity of players, the language of the court, and the unwritten rules that govern the playground. By analyzing key scenes that capture the essence of the LA playground culture, the chapter sets the stage for a deeper exploration of how "White Men Can't Jump" uses this setting to challenge and deconstruct stereotypes.

The Racial Dance: Sidney and Billy's Initial Confrontation

"White Men Can't Jump" opens with a humorous yet confrontational exchange between Sidney and Billy, addressing racial stereotypes head-on. This section explores the film's use of the initial confrontation between the characters to set the tone for its exploration of race. Through scene analysis, interviews with the actors, and discussions with cultural critics, we examine how the film uses humor to disarm and challenge racial preconceptions.

The section considers the verbal sparring between Sidney and Billy, marked by racial stereotypes and assumptions. It explores how the film navigates this delicate terrain, using humor to deconstruct stereotypes rather than reinforce them. The chapter also analyzes the body language, facial expressions, and comedic timing employed by Wesley Snipes and Woody Harrelson to infuse the scene with authenticity and satire. By unpacking the nuances of the racial dance between Sidney and Billy, the section provides insights into how "White Men Can't Jump" uses humor as a tool for cultural commentary.

Subverting Class Stereotypes: The Economic Realities of Pickup Basketball

Beyond race, the film also tackles class stereotypes by delving into the economic realities of the characters. This section explores how "White Men Can't Jump" uses the backdrop of pickup basketball to address class distinctions with humor and authenticity. Through scene analysis, interviews with the actors, and discussions with cultural critics, we examine the film's portrayal of economic disparities and how it subverts class stereotypes within the context of the sport.

The section considers the characters' relationships with money, from Billy's hustles to Sidney's street-smart approach to survival. It explores how the film depicts the economic struggles of the characters as they navigate the world of pickup basketball. The chapter also analyzes key scenes that showcase the characters' interactions with money and how these moments contribute to the film's broader social commentary. By unraveling the economic dynamics within the narrative, the section provides insights into how "White Men Can't Jump" uses humor to challenge class stereotypes.

Comedic Chemistry: Sidney and Billy as a Duo of Contrasts

The humor in "White Men Can't Jump" is heightened by the comedic chemistry between Sidney and Billy, two characters who are a study in contrasts. This section explores how the film uses their dynamic as a comedic duo to amplify its exploration of racial and class stereotypes. Through scene analysis, interviews with the actors, and discussions with the director, we examine the characters' contrasting backgrounds, personalities, and approaches to life.

The section delves into the banter, banter, and comedic timing that define Sidney and Billy's interactions. It explores how their differences become a source of humor, challenging both racial and class expectations. The chapter also analyzes key scenes that showcase the characters' comedic chemistry and how their contrasting qualities contribute to the film's overall comedic tone. By unpacking the dynamics of Sidney and

Billy's comedic partnership, the section provides readers with a deeper appreciation for how humor becomes a powerful tool for breaking down stereotypes.

Deconstructing Assumptions: The Game of Subversion on the Court

As Sidney and Billy team up on the court, "White Men Can't Jump" becomes a game of subversion, challenging assumptions about race and class. This section explores how the film uses the game of basketball as a metaphor for deconstructing societal stereotypes. Through scene analysis, interviews with the actors, and discussions with cultural critics, we examine the pivotal moments on the court where the characters defy expectations and challenge preconceptions.

The section considers how the film uses basketball as a level playing field where skill and intelligence trump stereotypes. It explores the characters' interactions with other players on the court, highlighting moments of subversion and cultural commentary. The chapter also analyzes key scenes that showcase the characters' basketball prowess as a means of challenging assumptions about their abilities. By unraveling the game of subversion on the court, the section provides insights into how "White Men Can't Jump" uses the sport to deconstruct societal stereotypes with wit and humor.

Sidney's Street Wisdom: Navigating Stereotypes with Humor

Wesley Snipes' portrayal of Sidney Deane infuses the character with street wisdom, using humor as a tool for navigating and challenging stereotypes. This section explores how Sidney's street-smart approach becomes a source of humor and authenticity within the film. Through scene analysis, interviews with the actor, and discussions with cultural critics, we examine Sidney's role as a subversive force, using humor to confront societal expectations.

The section considers how Sidney's street wisdom becomes a guiding force for both the character and the narrative. It explores the moments where Sidney uses humor to navigate racial and class dynamics, providing both levity and insight. The chapter also analyzes key scenes that showcase Sidney's street-smart humor and how it contributes to the film's broader social commentary. By unraveling the layers of Sidney's character, the section provides readers with a deeper understanding of how humor becomes a tool for challenging stereotypes.

Billy Hoyle's Conundrum: Navigating Racial Expectations

Woody Harrelson's portrayal of Billy Hoyle adds complexity to the film's exploration of racial stereotypes. This section examines how Billy's character navigates the conundrum of racial expectations with humor and authenticity. Through scene analysis, interviews with the actor, and discussions with cultural critics, we explore how Billy's journey becomes a central thread in the film's social commentary.

The section considers how Billy, as a white player in a predominantly black world, uses humor to challenge assumptions about his abilities. It explores the character's interactions with other players, the humor derived from his attempts to defy expectations, and the moments of self-awareness within the narrative. The chapter also analyzes key scenes that showcase Billy's navigation of racial expectations and how it contributes to the film's overall exploration of stereotypes. By unraveling the layers of Billy's character, the section provides readers with insights into how "White Men Can't Jump" uses humor to navigate the complexities of racial identity.

Cultural Resonance: Impact and Legacy in Racial Discourse

The impact of "White Men Can't Jump" extends beyond the realm of entertainment to contribute to broader discussions on race. This section explores the film's cultural resonance, examining its place in racial discourse and the enduring legacy of its exploration of stereotypes. Through reviews, audience reactions, and insights from cultural critics, we reflect on how the film has influenced conversations around race and stereotypes.

The section examines how critics and audiences responded to the film's nuanced approach to racial commentary. It considers the enduring popularity of "White Men Can't Jump" within the context of ongoing discussions on race in America. The chapter also reflects on the film's legacy and its contribution to the cinematic landscape of exploring race with humor and authenticity. By unpacking the cultural resonance, the section offers readers a comprehensive understanding of how "White Men Can't Jump" has left a lasting impact on racial discourse.

Conclusion: Humor as a Catalyst for Social Reflection

As we conclude our exploration of "Exploring Racial and Class Stereotypes with Humor," the chapter reflects on the transformative power of humor as a catalyst for social reflection. It considers how "White Men Can't Jump" masterfully uses wit, satire, and authenticity to navigate the complexities of racial and class stereotypes. Through cultural analysis, audience reactions, and discussions with film scholars, the section offers readers a final appreciation of the film's contribution to using humor as a tool for breaking down societal assumptions and challenging preconceptions.

Cult Following for Snipes and Harrelson's Chemistry

"White Men Can't Jump" has earned its place in the pantheon of cult classics, and much of its enduring appeal can be attributed to the magnetic chemistry between Wesley Snipes and Woody Harrelson. In this section, we explore the factors that have led to the film's cult following, delving into the on-screen magic created by Snipes and Harrelson and its impact on the movie's cultural legacy. Through scene analysis, interviews with the actors, and discussions with cultural critics, we unravel the nuances of their chemistry and the unique elements that have contributed to the film's cult status.

The Birth of an Unlikely Duo: Snipes and Harrelson's Casting Alchemy

The chemistry between Wesley Snipes and Woody Harrelson is the beating heart of "White Men Can't Jump," and it all begins with their casting. This section explores the casting process that brought these two actors together and the alchemy that defined their dynamic on screen. Through interviews with the casting director, the director Ron Shelton, and the actors themselves, we unravel the story of how Snipes and Harrelson, each known for their distinct styles, were chosen to play Sidney Deane and Billy Hoyle.

The section considers the initial reactions to the casting choices, both from the filmmakers and the actors themselves. It delves into how the director envisioned this unlikely duo and the qualities that each actor brought to their respective roles. By analyzing key scenes that showcase the actors' early interactions on screen, the chapter sets the stage for understanding the casting alchemy that laid the foundation for the enduring chemistry between Snipes and Harrelson.

On-Screen Magic: The Dynamic Partnership of Sidney and Billy

Once on set, Snipes and Harrelson brought Sidney and Billy to life with a dynamic partnership that became the soul of the film. This section explores the on-screen magic created by the actors, diving into their performances and the nuances of their dynamic partnership. Through scene analysis, interviews with the actors, and discussions with the director, we unravel the layers of Sidney and Billy's relationship and the authentic chemistry that defines their on-screen interactions.

The section considers how Snipes and Harrelson approached their roles and the moments where their performances truly clicked. It explores the evolution of Sidney and Billy's relationship on screen, from initial rivalry to a genuine friendship. The chapter also analyzes key scenes that showcase the actors' ability to play off each other's energy and elevate the humor and authenticity of their on-screen dynamic. By unpacking the nuances of Sidney and Billy's partnership, the section provides readers with a deeper appreciation for the on-screen magic that makes "White Men Can't Jump" a cult classic.

Capturing Lightning in a Bottle: The Improvisational Spirit

Part of what makes the chemistry between Snipes and Harrelson so special is the improvisational spirit they brought to their performances. This section explores how the actors captured lightning in a bottle by infusing spontaneity and humor into their scenes. Through interviews with the actors, discussions with the director, and insights from comedy experts, we examine the performative chemistry that elevated the film's comedic elements.

The section delves into the actors' approach to improvisation and how it added authenticity and unpredictability to their performances. It explores key scenes that showcase Snipes and Harrelson's ability to play with the script, adding unexpected moments of humor and camaraderie. The chapter also considers the director's role in fostering an environment that allowed for creative spontaneity on set. By analyzing the improvisational spirit that permeates the film, the section offers readers insights into the magic that occurs when two talented actors are given room to bring their characters to life with authenticity and humor.

The Banter and Bickering: Snipes and Harrelson's Comic Timing

At the heart of Sidney and Billy's dynamic is the banter and bickering that define their relationship. This section explores how Snipes and Harrelson masterfully navigated the comedic timing of their characters, turning witty exchanges into memorable moments. Through scene analysis, interviews with the actors, and discussions with comedy experts, we examine the linguistic nuances of their banter and the impeccable timing that adds a layer of humor to their dynamic.

The section considers the role of banter in conveying the characters' personalities and the dynamics of their relationship. It explores how Snipes and Harrelson used their comic timing to bring authenticity to the humor in the film, enhancing the overall comedic tone. The chapter also analyzes key scenes that showcase the actors' banter and bickering, providing insights into the nuances of their comic timing. By unraveling the linguistic dynamics of Sidney and Billy's relationship, the section offers readers a deeper appreciation for the comedic elements that contribute to the film's cult status.

The Underlying Friendship: Snipes and Harrelson's Authentic Connection

Beneath the banter and humor, "White Men Can't Jump" also captures the essence of a genuine friendship between Sidney and Billy. This section explores how Snipes and Harrelson conveyed the underlying friendship of their characters, adding emotional depth to the film. Through interviews with the actors, discussions with the director, and insights from film scholars, we examine the authenticity of the connection between Snipes and Harrelson on screen.

The section considers the moments where the actors conveyed the vulnerability and sincerity of Sidney and Billy's friendship. It explores the evolution of their relationship, from initial skepticism to a bond forged through shared experiences. The chapter also analyzes key scenes that showcase the actors' ability to convey the emotional nuances of friendship, providing readers with insights into the authentic connection that lies at the heart of "White Men Can't Jump."

Cultural Impact: Sidney and Billy's Enduring Legacy

The cultural impact of "White Men Can't Jump" extends beyond its initial release, and Sidney and Billy have become iconic characters in the realm of sports cinema. This section explores how the chemistry between Snipes and Harrelson contributed to the enduring legacy of the film. Through reviews, audience reactions, and insights from cultural critics, we reflect on the impact of Sidney and Billy's dynamic partnership on the broader cultural landscape.

The section examines how critics and audiences responded to the chemistry between Snipes and Harrelson, praising their performances as integral to the film's success. It considers the enduring popularity of Sidney and Billy as characters within the context of sports cinema. The chapter also reflects on the film's legacy and its contribution to the cinematic landscape of buddy comedies. By unpacking the cultural impact, the section offers readers a comprehensive understanding of how the chemistry between Snipes and Harrelson has left an indelible mark on the legacy of "White Men Can't Jump."

Fandom and Memorable Moments: Celebrating the Cult Following

The cult following of "White Men Can't Jump" is fueled by fandom and the memorable moments created by Snipes and Harrelson. This section explores how the film has become a cultural touchstone, celebrated by fans who appreciate the unique chemistry between the actors. Through fan testimonials, discussions with cultural critics, and reflections on memorable scenes, we delve into the factors that have contributed to the film's enduring cult status.

The section considers the emergence of catchphrases, iconic scenes, and memorable quotes that have become synonymous with the film's legacy. It explores fan communities, social media discussions, and the ways in which audiences continue to celebrate and revisit the film. The chapter also reflects on the enduring popularity of "White Men Can't Jump" as a source of nostalgia and entertainment. By unraveling the elements that contribute to the film's cult following, the section offers readers insights into the enduring appeal of Sidney and Billy's dynamic partnership.

Conclusion: Snipes and Harrelson's Timeless Chemistry

As we conclude our exploration of "Cult Following for Snipes and Harrelson's Chemistry," the chapter reflects on the timeless chemistry between Wesley Snipes and Woody Harrelson that continues to resonate with audiences. It considers how their dynamic partnership, infused with authenticity, humor, and a touch of streetwise charm, has left an indelible mark on the cultural legacy of "White Men Can't Jump." Through cultural analysis, fan testimonials, and discussions with film scholars, the section offers readers a final appreciation of the actors' contribution to the rich tapestry of basketball-themed movies, celebrating the enduring and timeless chemistry that defines Sidney and Billy's unforgettable bond.

Chapter 6 - Coach Carter (2005)
Bringing the Story of Ken Carter's Crusade to Screen

"Coach Carter" stands as a cinematic testament to the transformative power of mentorship, discipline, and the unwavering belief in the potential of every individual. This section explores the journey of bringing Ken Carter's crusade to the screen, examining the creative choices, casting decisions, and the collaborative effort that resulted in a film that not only depicts a gripping sports story but also addresses important themes of education, resilience, and personal growth.

The Genesis of the Project: Adapting the Real-Life Saga of Coach Carter

Before "Coach Carter" graced the silver screen, it was a real-life saga that captured attention. This section explores the genesis of the project, from the initial inspiration drawn from Ken Carter's story to the decision to adapt it into a feature film. Through interviews with the filmmakers, discussions with the screenwriter, and insights from the real Coach Carter, we delve into the process of translating a compelling real-life narrative into a cinematic experience.

The section considers the motivations behind choosing Coach Carter's story, examining how his unconventional coaching methods and commitment to academics resonated with filmmakers. It explores the challenges of adapting a true story for the screen, balancing the need for dramatic elements with a commitment to authenticity. By analyzing key moments in the narrative that shaped the film's direction, the chapter sets the stage for understanding the challenges and rewards of bringing Ken Carter's crusade to the screen.

Casting the Crusader: Samuel L. Jackson as Coach Ken Carter

One of the pivotal decisions in bringing Coach Carter's story to life was the casting of the titular character. This section explores the casting process and the selection of Samuel L. Jackson to embody the crusader Coach Ken Carter. Through interviews with the casting director, discussions with the director, and insights from Samuel L. Jackson himself, we unravel the considerations that led to this casting choice and the impact it had on the film.

The section delves into how Jackson approached the role, capturing not just Coach Carter's outward demeanor but also delving into the nuances of his character. It explores the actor's commitment to authenticity, capturing the essence of the real-life coach. The chapter also analyzes key scenes that showcase Jackson's portrayal of Coach Carter and the transformative effect it had on the film. By unpacking the casting process, the section provides readers with insights into the deliberate choices that shaped the character of Coach Ken Carter on screen.

Balancing Drama and Reality: Scripting the High School Hoops Drama

Crafting the screenplay for "Coach Carter" required a delicate balance between the dramatic elements necessary for compelling storytelling and the reality of the events it sought to depict. This section explores the scripting process, examining the challenges of capturing the essence of Coach Carter's crusade while infusing the narrative with the necessary cinematic elements. Through interviews with the screenwriter, discussions with the director, and insights from Coach Carter, we delve into the creative decisions that shaped the screenplay.

The section considers how the screenplay navigated key moments in the narrative, from the controversial lockout decision to the academic emphasis that defined Coach Carter's coaching philosophy. It explores the collaborative effort between the screenwriter and the filmmakers to ensure that the film resonated not just as a sports drama but as a story of personal growth and societal challenges. By analyzing pivotal scenes that highlight the delicate balance between drama and reality, the chapter offers readers a comprehensive understanding of the choices made in scripting the high school hoops drama of "Coach Carter."

On-Set Dynamics: Capturing the Spirit of Richmond High School

Filming "Coach Carter" required not just a talented cast and crew but also an understanding of the unique dynamics of Richmond High School and its community. This section explores the on-set dynamics, examining the efforts made to capture the spirit of the real-life setting. Through interviews with the director, discussions with the cinematographer, and insights from the actors, we unravel the strategies employed to create an authentic and immersive on-screen representation of Richmond High.

The section considers how the filmmakers collaborated with the school and its community, incorporating real students and athletes into the film. It explores the challenges of filming in an actual high school and the advantages it brought to the authenticity of the narrative. The chapter also analyzes key scenes that showcase the on-set dynamics, providing readers with insights into the efforts made to capture the spirit of Richmond High School and its impact on the film's overall authenticity.

Beyond the Locker Room: Exploring Coach Carter's Impact Beyond Basketball

"Coach Carter" transcends the boundaries of a traditional sports drama by addressing broader themes of education, discipline, and personal responsibility. This section explores how the film goes beyond the locker room, examining the narrative choices that emphasize Coach Carter's impact on the lives of his players beyond the basketball court. Through interviews with the director, discussions with the screenwriter, and insights from Coach Carter himself, we delve into the intentional decisions that transformed the film into a story of mentorship and resilience.

The section considers how the film navigates the challenges faced by the characters, both academically and personally, and how Coach Carter's guidance becomes a driving force for positive change. It explores the deliberate choices made to depict the players' struggles and triumphs, emphasizing the importance of education and self-discipline. By analyzing key moments in the narrative that go beyond the traditional sports drama tropes, the chapter provides readers with insights into the thematic depth that elevates "Coach Carter" into a film that resonates with audiences far beyond the realm of basketball.

Music and Motivation: Crafting the Film's Soundtrack

The soundtrack of "Coach Carter" contributes to the emotional and motivational journey of the characters. This section explores the crafting of the film's soundtrack, examining the musical choices that enhance the cinematic experience. Through interviews with the music supervisor, discussions with the director, and insights from the composers, we unravel the considerations that went into selecting the songs that accompany the narrative.

The section considers how the music complements the emotional beats of the film, enhancing moments of triumph, struggle, and personal growth. It explores the collaborative effort between the filmmakers and musicians to create a soundtrack that resonates with the themes of mentorship, discipline, and resilience. The chapter also analyzes key scenes where the soundtrack plays a pivotal role in conveying the emotional depth of the narrative. By unpacking the musical elements, the section provides readers with insights into how the film's soundtrack becomes a powerful tool for conveying the motivations and emotions of Coach Carter and his players.

Critical Reception: Coach Carter's Impact on Audience and Critics

"Coach Carter" received a varied reception from both audiences and critics, with praise for its inspirational narrative and critique for its adherence to sports drama conventions. This section explores the critical reception of the film, examining how it resonated with different audiences and the thematic elements that drew both acclaim and criticism. Through reviews, audience reactions, and insights from film scholars, we reflect on the film's impact on the cinematic landscape and its place within the sports drama genre.

The section considers the themes that struck a chord with audiences, including mentorship, discipline, and the pursuit of education. It also explores the critiques, including the film's adherence to certain sports drama tropes and its approach to representing the real-life events. The chapter provides a nuanced analysis of how "Coach Carter" navigated the expectations of both critics and audiences, offering readers a comprehensive understanding of the film's reception and its lasting impact.

Legacy and Influence: Coach Carter's Enduring Impact

Beyond its initial release, "Coach Carter" has left a lasting legacy, inspiring audiences and becoming a staple in discussions about sports dramas with a social message. This section explores the legacy and influence of "Coach Carter," examining how the film continues to resonate with audiences and its enduring impact on the sports drama genre. Through reflections from the filmmakers, discussions with film scholars, and insights from Coach Carter himself, we unravel the factors that have contributed to the film's enduring influence.

The section considers how the themes of mentorship, discipline, and the pursuit of education continue to make "Coach Carter" relevant. It explores the film's impact on discussions about sports dramas that tackle social issues and its place within the broader landscape of inspirational cinema. The chapter also reflects on the film's enduring popularity and its role in shaping the narrative of coaches who go beyond the game. By unpacking the legacy and influence, the section offers readers a final appreciation of how "Coach Carter" has become more than a sports drama—it's a story of enduring inspiration.

Conclusion: Coach Carter's Enduring Crusade on Screen

As we conclude our exploration of "Bringing the Story of Ken Carter's Crusade to Screen," the chapter reflects on the enduring crusade of Coach Carter on screen. It considers how the filmmakers, through deliberate choices in casting, scripting, and thematic exploration, transformed a real-life saga into a cinematic experience that goes beyond the confines of a traditional sports drama. Through critical analysis, insights from the filmmakers, and reflections on the film's legacy, the section offers readers a final appreciation of how "Coach Carter" stands as a testament to the transformative power of mentorship, education, and unwavering belief in the potential of every individual.

Samuel L. Jackson Leads with Gravitas and Inspiration

In the realm of sports dramas, casting is a pivotal factor that can make or break the portrayal of real-life stories. When it comes to "Coach Carter," the casting of Samuel L. Jackson in the titular role brings a level of gravitas and inspiration that elevates the film beyond the typical sports narrative. This section delves into the impact of Samuel L. Jackson's portrayal, exploring how his performance as Coach Ken Carter contributes to the film's resonance and the enduring inspiration it provides to audiences.

Crafting the Persona: Samuel L. Jackson as Coach Ken Carter

Samuel L. Jackson is known for his commanding presence and versatility as an actor, but his portrayal of Coach Ken Carter adds a layer of depth to his repertoire. This section explores how Jackson crafted the persona of Coach Carter, diving into the nuances of his performance. Through interviews with the actor, discussions with the director, and insights from Coach Carter himself, we unravel the considerations and choices that went into creating a character that goes beyond the traditional sports movie archetype.

The section considers how Jackson approached the role, capturing the essence of Coach Carter's leadership style, discipline, and commitment to his players. It explores the actor's preparation process, including interactions with the real Coach Carter and observations of his coaching style. The chapter also analyzes key scenes that showcase Jackson's portrayal, providing readers with insights into the authenticity and gravitas he brings to the character. By unpacking the crafting of Coach Carter's persona, the section offers readers a deeper appreciation for the actor's contribution to the film.

The Gravitas of Leadership: Jackson's Commanding Presence

Coach Ken Carter is not just a basketball coach; he is a leader, mentor, and disciplinarian. Samuel L. Jackson's commanding presence on screen adds a layer of gravitas to the character, reinforcing the leadership qualities that define Coach Carter. This section explores how Jackson's portrayal conveys the gravitas of leadership, examining the moments where his on-screen presence becomes a powerful force within the narrative. Through scene analysis, interviews with the actor, and insights from the director, we delve into the intentional choices that highlight Jackson's command as Coach Carter.

The section considers the scenes where Jackson's presence is particularly impactful, whether in the locker room, the classroom, or on the basketball court. It explores how the actor embodies the authority and strength that Coach Carter exudes, emphasizing the discipline and expectations he sets for his players. The chapter also reflects on the collaborative effort between the actor and the director to ensure that Jackson's commanding presence aligns with the real-life persona of Coach Carter. By analyzing the moments of leadership gravitas, the section provides readers with a nuanced understanding of how Jackson's performance elevates the character and the overall impact of "Coach Carter."

Inspirational Mentorship: Jackson's Approach to Coaching Philosophy

Central to Coach Carter's character is his commitment to being more than just a basketball coach—he is an inspirational mentor with a profound coaching philosophy. This section explores how Samuel L. Jackson approached the depiction of Coach Carter's mentorship, examining the nuances of his coaching philosophy and the inspirational impact it has on the characters and the audience. Through interviews with the actor, discussions with the director, and insights from Coach Carter, we unravel the intentional choices that showcase Jackson's approach to portraying the inspirational mentorship at the core of the film.

The section considers how Jackson conveys Coach Carter's emphasis on education, discipline, and personal responsibility. It explores the scenes that capture the mentor-mentee dynamics, examining the actor's ability to inspire and guide his players both on and off the court. The chapter also reflects on the collaborative effort between the actor and the real Coach Carter to ensure an authentic representation of the coaching philosophy. By analyzing the moments of inspirational mentorship, the section provides readers with insights into Jackson's portrayal of Coach Carter as a figure of lasting inspiration.

Navigating Tough Decisions: Jackson's Portrayal of Carter's Lockout

One of the most pivotal moments in "Coach Carter" is Coach Carter's controversial decision to enforce a lockout due to his players' academic shortcomings. Samuel L. Jackson's portrayal adds layers of complexity to this challenging decision, showcasing the internal struggles and conviction that define

Coach Carter's character. This section explores how Jackson navigates the tough decisions of the lockout, examining the emotional depth he brings to the character during this critical juncture. Through scene analysis, interviews with the actor, and insights from Coach Carter, we delve into the intentional choices that highlight Jackson's portrayal of the lockout and its impact on the narrative.

The section considers the nuances of Jackson's performance during the lockout scenes, capturing the internal conflict, frustration, and unwavering belief in the long-term benefits of his decision. It explores how the actor conveys Coach Carter's commitment to prioritizing education over immediate athletic success and the toll it takes on him as a leader. The chapter also reflects on the collaborative effort between the actor, the director, and the real Coach Carter to ensure an authentic representation of this pivotal moment. By analyzing Jackson's portrayal of tough decisions, the section provides readers with a deeper understanding of the emotional complexities woven into Coach Carter's character.

Fatherly Guidance: Jackson's Portrayal of Personal Connection

Beyond the role of a coach, Coach Carter serves as a fatherly figure, providing guidance and support to his players in their personal lives. Samuel L. Jackson's portrayal adds a layer of personal connection and warmth to this aspect of Coach Carter's character. This section explores how Jackson conveys the fatherly guidance that defines Coach Carter's relationships with his players, examining the moments of personal connection that go beyond the basketball court. Through interviews with the actor, discussions with the director, and insights from Coach Carter, we unravel the intentional choices that showcase Jackson's approach to portraying the personal connection at the heart of the film.

The section considers the scenes where Jackson's portrayal captures the fatherly dynamics, exploring the actor's ability to convey care, concern, and encouragement. It delves into the emotional nuances of the relationships between Coach Carter and his players, showcasing how Jackson's performance adds a layer of depth to the narrative. The chapter also reflects on the collaborative effort between the actor and the real Coach Carter to ensure an authentic representation of these personal connections. By analyzing Jackson's portrayal of fatherly guidance, the section provides readers with insights into the emotional richness that defines the relationships within "Coach Carter."

Challenges and Triumphs: Jackson's Portrayal of Personal Growth

"Coach Carter" is not just a sports drama; it's a story of personal growth, both for the players and the coach. Samuel L. Jackson's portrayal captures the challenges and triumphs of Coach Carter's own journey, adding a layer of vulnerability and resilience to the character. This section explores how Jackson conveys the personal growth of Coach Carter, examining the moments of struggle and triumph that define his character arc. Through scene analysis, interviews with the actor, and insights from Coach Carter, we delve into the intentional choices that showcase Jackson's approach to portraying the challenges and triumphs of personal growth.

The section considers the scenes where Jackson's portrayal captures the vulnerability of Coach Carter, exploring the actor's ability to convey the emotional highs and lows of the character's journey. It examines how the actor navigates the moments of self-reflection, redemption, and the ultimate triumphs that define Coach Carter's evolution. The chapter also reflects on the collaborative effort between the actor and the director to ensure an authentic representation of this personal growth. By analyzing Jackson's portrayal of challenges and triumphs, the section provides readers with insights into the emotional complexity that adds depth to the character of Coach Carter.

Legacy of Leadership: Jackson's Contribution to "Coach Carter's" Enduring Impact

As we explore Samuel L. Jackson's contribution to "Coach Carter," it becomes evident that his portrayal of Coach Ken Carter is a defining factor in the film's enduring impact. This section reflects on the legacy of leadership that Jackson brings to the character, examining how his performance contributes to the film's lasting influence. Through critical analysis, insights from the actor, and reflections on the film's legacy, we unravel the factors that make Jackson's contribution a crucial element in the enduring impact of "Coach Carter."

The section considers how Jackson's portrayal of Coach Carter aligns with the real-life persona of the coach, emphasizing the authenticity and resonance of his performance. It explores the thematic elements that Jackson brings to the forefront, including leadership, mentorship, and the pursuit of personal and academic excellence. The chapter also reflects on the collaborative effort between the actor and the real Coach Carter to ensure a portrayal that reflects the coach's impact beyond the basketball court. By analyzing Jackson's legacy of leadership, the section provides readers with a final appreciation of how his contribution has solidified "Coach Carter" as more than a sports drama—it's a story of enduring inspiration.

Emphasizing Education Alongside Athletic Dreams

In the world of sports dramas, where triumphs on the field often take center stage, "Coach Carter" distinguishes itself by placing a spotlight on a critical aspect that transcends the basketball court: education. This section delves into how the film, under the guidance of Coach Ken Carter, emphasizes the importance of education alongside the pursuit of athletic dreams. Through scene analysis, insights from the real Coach Carter, and reflections from the filmmakers, we explore the intentional choices that shape the narrative, making "Coach Carter" not just a sports drama but a story that underscores the value of academic excellence.

Setting the Stage: Richmond High School and Its Challenges

Before delving into the emphasis on education, it's crucial to understand the context in which Coach Carter's story unfolds. This section explores the setting of Richmond High School, a place marked by socio-economic challenges, limited resources, and a pervasive narrative that sees sports as the only viable path to success. Through an analysis of key scenes, discussions with the filmmakers, and insights from Coach Carter, we unravel how the film establishes the challenges faced by the students and the systemic issues that impact their educational journeys.

The section considers how the setting contributes to the urgency of Coach Carter's mission to instill the value of education. It explores the societal expectations placed on young athletes and the limited opportunities that seem available to them. By examining scenes that portray the school's environment, the chapter provides readers with a foundational understanding of the uphill battle Coach Carter faces in emphasizing education alongside athletic dreams.

Coach Carter's Philosophy: Education as Non-Negotiable

Central to Coach Carter's character is a philosophy that challenges the status quo: education is non-negotiable. This section explores how the film articulates Coach Carter's unwavering commitment to academic excellence, establishing it as a fundamental principle rather than a secondary consideration. Through interviews with the real Coach Carter, discussions with the screenwriter, and scene analysis, we delve into the narrative choices that define education as a core aspect of Coach Carter's coaching philosophy.

The section considers pivotal scenes where Coach Carter articulates his expectations regarding academics. It explores how the character communicates the idea that education is not just a means to an end but an end in itself—an essential element in shaping the future of his players. The chapter also reflects on the collaborative effort between the filmmakers and the real Coach Carter to ensure an authentic representation of the coach's commitment to education. By analyzing key moments that establish Coach Carter's philosophy, the section provides readers with insights into how the film positions education at the forefront of the narrative.

Academic Accountability: The Lockout Decision

One of the defining moments in "Coach Carter" is the controversial decision to enforce a lockout due to the players' academic underperformance. This section explores how the lockout becomes a powerful narrative device, symbolizing Coach Carter's uncompromising stance on academic accountability. Through scene analysis, insights from the real Coach Carter, and discussions with the filmmakers, we unravel the nuances of this critical decision and its impact on the players and the overarching theme of education.

The section considers the lead-up to the lockout decision, examining how the film portrays the players' academic struggles and the internal conflict within Coach Carter. It explores the scene where the lockout is enforced, showcasing the emotional weight of the decision and its repercussions. The chapter also reflects on the collaborative effort between the filmmakers and the real Coach Carter to ensure an authentic representation of the challenges surrounding academic accountability. By analyzing the lockout decision, the section provides readers with insights into how the film uses this pivotal moment to underscore the importance of education.

Beyond the Classroom: Education as a Lifelong Pursuit

"Coach Carter" goes beyond presenting education as a means to an end within the context of high school. This section explores how the film conveys the idea that education is a lifelong pursuit, with ramifications that extend far beyond the confines of the classroom. Through interviews with the actors, discussions with the director, and scene analysis, we delve into the narrative choices that depict education as a transformative and enduring aspect of the characters' lives.

The section considers scenes that highlight the players' journeys beyond high school, showcasing how the lessons learned in Coach Carter's classroom continue to shape their paths. It explores the characters' decisions to pursue higher education and the impact of their commitment to academic excellence on their futures. The chapter also reflects on the collaborative effort between the filmmakers and the real Coach Carter to ensure an authentic representation of the long-term impact of education. By analyzing scenes that depict education as a lifelong pursuit, the section provides readers with insights into how the film encourages a broader perspective on the value of academic achievement.

Challenges and Resistance: Navigating Societal Expectations

Emphasizing education in an environment where societal expectations prioritize athletic success poses its own set of challenges. This section explores how "Coach Carter" navigates the resistance faced by the characters as they challenge prevailing norms and expectations. Through scene analysis, interviews with the actors, and insights from the real Coach Carter, we unravel the complexities of navigating societal expectations and the resistance encountered when prioritizing education.

The section considers scenes that depict the characters facing resistance from their peers, families, and even the community. It explores the societal pressures that push back against the idea of prioritizing education over immediate athletic success. The chapter also reflects on the collaborative effort between the filmmakers and the real Coach Carter to ensure an authentic representation of the challenges faced by the characters. By analyzing scenes that portray challenges and resistance, the section provides readers with insights into the broader social context that shapes the film's emphasis on education.

Counseling Beyond the Court: Coach Carter as a Mentor

Coach Carter's role as a mentor extends beyond the basketball court, encompassing academic guidance and counseling. This section explores how the film portrays Coach Carter's efforts to provide holistic mentorship, offering academic support and guidance to his players. Through scene analysis, insights from the real Coach Carter, and discussions with the actors, we delve into the moments that showcase Coach Carter as a mentor who is invested in the academic success and personal growth of his players.

The section considers scenes where Coach Carter provides academic guidance, counseling his players on the importance of making the right choices in their academic pursuits. It explores the character's commitment to addressing not only their athletic ambitions but also their broader life goals. The chapter also reflects on the collaborative effort between the filmmakers and the real Coach Carter to ensure an authentic representation of mentorship beyond the court. By analyzing scenes that highlight Coach Carter's role as a mentor, the section provides readers with insights into the multifaceted guidance he provides to his players.

Parental Involvement: Shifting Perspectives on Education

"Coach Carter" also explores the dynamics of parental involvement in the educational journeys of the players. This section delves into how the film depicts the shifting perspectives of parents and guardians, emphasizing the transformative impact of Coach Carter's approach to education. Through interviews with the actors, discussions with the director, and scene analysis, we explore the narrative choices that portray the evolution of parental perspectives on education.

The section considers scenes where parents and guardians initially resist Coach Carter's emphasis on academics but undergo a transformation in their understanding. It explores how the film depicts the characters' realization of the long-term benefits of prioritizing education. The chapter also reflects on the collaborative effort between the filmmakers and the real Coach Carter to ensure an authentic representation of the evolving parental perspectives. By analyzing scenes that depict parental involvement, the section provides readers with insights into the film's portrayal of the broader impact of emphasizing education.

Academic Triumphs: Celebrating Achievements Beyond the Court

"Coach Carter" reaches its crescendo not just with on-court victories but also with academic triumphs. This section explores how the film celebrates the characters' academic achievements as integral to their overall success. Through scene analysis, interviews with the actors, and insights from the real Coach Carter, we delve into the moments that showcase the academic triumphs of the players and the broader message of the film regarding the intersection of sports and education.

The section considers scenes that depict the characters excelling academically, showcasing how their commitment to education pays off in the form of achievements beyond the basketball court. It explores how the film communicates the idea that academic success is a powerful catalyst for personal and community transformation. The chapter also reflects on the collaborative effort between the filmmakers and the real Coach Carter to ensure an authentic representation of academic triumphs. By analyzing scenes that celebrate academic achievements, the section provides readers with insights into the film's ultimate message regarding the intertwining paths of sports and education.

Legacy of Educational Emphasis: Coach Carter's Lasting Impact

As we conclude our exploration of "Emphasizing Education Alongside Athletic Dreams," the section reflects on the lasting impact of Coach Carter's approach to education. It considers how the film's emphasis on academic excellence has contributed to its enduring legacy. Through critical analysis, insights from the real Coach Carter, and reflections on the film's impact, we unravel the factors that make the educational message of "Coach Carter" a crucial element in the film's enduring influence.

The section reflects on how the film's narrative choices regarding education align with the real-life philosophy of Coach Carter. It explores the broader implications of emphasizing education within the sports drama genre and the impact it has had on audiences. The chapter also considers the collaborative effort between the filmmakers and the real Coach Carter to ensure an authentic representation of the coach's commitment to education. By analyzing the legacy of educational emphasis, the section provides readers with a final appreciation of how "Coach Carter" stands as a unique sports drama that goes beyond the court, leaving a lasting impact through its powerful message on the importance of education.

Wrestling With Sports Movie Tropes and Clichés

In the vast landscape of sports movies, there exists a tapestry of tropes and clichés that often define the genre. "Coach Carter," while firmly rooted in the traditions of sports dramas, distinguishes itself by navigating and, at times, challenging these well-worn conventions. This section explores how the film engages with and wrestles against sports movie tropes and clichés, offering a fresh perspective on the genre. Through scene analysis, interviews with the filmmakers, and insights from the real Coach Carter, we unravel the intentional choices that set "Coach Carter" apart as a nuanced exploration of both sports and societal expectations.

Establishing the Underdog Narrative: Subverting and Reinforcing Expectations

Sports movies are renowned for their underdog narratives, where a team or individual rises from obscurity to achieve greatness. "Coach Carter" begins with the familiar premise of an underdog team in a challenging environment. This section explores how the film both subverts and reinforces the underdog narrative, setting the stage for a more complex examination of success and failure. Through scene analysis, discussions with the screenwriter, and insights from Coach Carter, we delve into the intentional choices that shape the underdog narrative in the film.

The section considers scenes that establish the underdog status of the Richmond High School basketball team, exploring how the film plays with audience expectations. It analyzes moments that subvert traditional underdog tropes, offering a more nuanced portrayal of success and failure. The chapter also reflects on the collaborative effort between the filmmakers and the real Coach Carter to ensure an authentic representation of the challenges faced by the team. By analyzing the establishment of the underdog narrative, the section provides readers with insights into how "Coach Carter" navigates the conventions of sports movie storytelling.

The Mentor-Student Dynamic: Beyond Clichéd Coaching Tropes

A staple of sports movies is the mentor-student dynamic between the coach and the players, often laden with clichéd coaching tropes. This section explores how "Coach Carter" transcends these clichés by presenting a mentorship that extends beyond the basketball court. Through scene analysis, interviews with the actors, and insights from the real Coach Carter, we unravel the intentional choices that distinguish the mentor-student dynamic in the film.

The section considers scenes that depict Coach Carter's mentorship, exploring how the film delves into the personal lives and academic pursuits of the players. It analyzes moments that go beyond the traditional coach-player relationship, showcasing the multifaceted guidance provided by Coach Carter. The chapter also reflects on the collaborative effort between the filmmakers and the real Coach Carter to ensure an authentic representation of mentorship dynamics. By examining the mentor-student dynamic, the section provides readers with insights into how "Coach Carter" challenges and expands the conventions of coaching tropes in sports movies.

Balancing Athletics and Academics: Challenging the Singular Focus Trope

A recurring trope in sports movies is the singular focus on athletic achievement, often overshadowing other aspects of characters' lives. "Coach Carter" takes a different approach by challenging this trope, emphasizing the importance of balancing athletics and academics. This section explores how the film navigates the delicate balance between sports and education, offering a more holistic perspective on the lives of its characters. Through scene analysis, discussions with the screenwriter, and insights from Coach Carter, we unravel the intentional choices that challenge the singular focus trope in the film.

The section considers scenes that depict the characters juggling their athletic pursuits with academic responsibilities, showcasing the challenges of maintaining this balance. It analyzes moments that emphasize the consequences of neglecting academics, challenging the traditional notion of sports success as the sole measure of achievement. The chapter also reflects on the collaborative effort between the filmmakers and the real Coach Carter to ensure an authentic representation of the challenges faced by student-athletes. By examining the balancing act between athletics and academics, the section provides readers with insights into how "Coach Carter" subverts expectations regarding the singular focus trope in sports movies.

The Redemption Arc: Complexities Beyond the Cliché

Redemption arcs are a common feature in sports movies, where characters overcome personal challenges to achieve redemption through athletic success. This section explores how "Coach Carter" introduces complexities beyond the clichéd redemption narrative, presenting a more nuanced exploration of personal growth and redemption. Through scene analysis, interviews with the actors, and insights from the real Coach Carter, we delve into the intentional choices that shape the redemption arcs in the film.

The section considers scenes that depict characters facing personal challenges and striving for redemption, exploring the complexities of their journeys. It analyzes moments that go beyond the traditional narrative arc, showcasing the layers of personal growth and the acknowledgment that redemption is not always tied to on-court triumphs. The chapter also reflects on the collaborative effort between the filmmakers and the real Coach Carter to ensure an authentic representation of the complexities of redemption. By examining the redemption arcs in the film, the section provides readers with insights into how "Coach Carter" adds depth to this common sports movie trope.

Team Unity and Diversity: Moving Beyond Stereotypes

Team unity and diversity are recurrent themes in sports movies, often depicted through characters who overcome differences to form a cohesive unit. This section explores how "Coach Carter" moves beyond stereotypes by presenting a diverse group of characters with unique backgrounds and challenges. Through scene analysis, discussions with the screenwriter, and insights from Coach Carter, we unravel the intentional choices that contribute to a more authentic portrayal of team unity and diversity in the film.

The section considers scenes that showcase the diverse backgrounds and challenges of the players, exploring how the film moves beyond superficial portrayals of unity. It analyzes moments that challenge stereotypes and celebrate the individuality of each character, highlighting the importance of embracing diversity within the team. The chapter also reflects on the collaborative effort between the filmmakers and the real Coach Carter to ensure an authentic representation of the complexities of team dynamics. By examining team unity and diversity, the section provides readers with insights into how "Coach Carter" goes beyond the clichés associated with these themes in sports movies.

The Big Game Moment: Rethinking Success and Failure

In many sports movies, the climax often centers around a big game or championship, where success or failure is measured by the outcome on the field. This section explores how "Coach Carter" rethinks the conventional approach to the big game moment, presenting a more nuanced perspective on success and failure. Through scene analysis, interviews with the filmmakers, and insights from the real Coach Carter, we delve into the intentional choices that shape the climactic moments in the film.

The section considers scenes that lead up to and depict the big game, exploring how the film challenges the idea that success is solely determined by victory on the court. It analyzes moments that redefine success and failure, showcasing the broader life lessons learned by the characters. The chapter also reflects on the collaborative effort between the filmmakers and the real Coach Carter to ensure an authentic representation of the complexities associated with defining success. By examining the big game moment, the section provides readers with insights into how "Coach Carter" subverts expectations regarding success and failure in sports movies.

Legacy Beyond the Trophy: Rethinking the Enduring Impact

The conclusion of many sports movies often involves a symbolic trophy or championship, signaling the ultimate triumph for the characters. This section explores how "Coach Carter" rethinks the idea of a legacy beyond the trophy, presenting a more profound consideration of the enduring impact of the characters' journeys. Through critical analysis, discussions with the screenwriter, and reflections on the film's impact, we unravel the factors that make the conclusion of "Coach Carter" a unique departure from traditional sports movie endings.

The section reflects on the legacy left by the characters, considering how their individual journeys contribute to a broader narrative of personal and community transformation. It explores the film's emphasis on the enduring impact of the lessons learned, going beyond the immediate triumphs or failures. The chapter also reflects on the collaborative effort between the filmmakers and the real Coach Carter to ensure an authentic representation of the lasting legacy of the characters. By examining the legacy beyond the trophy, the section provides readers with a final appreciation of how "Coach Carter" challenges and redefines the traditional conclusion of sports movies.

In conclusion, "Coach Carter" stands as a compelling exploration of sports and societal expectations, not only through its narrative but also through its intentional engagement with and wrestling against sports movie tropes and clichés. The film's ability to subvert expectations, present nuanced character dynamics, and offer a more profound consideration of success and failure contributes to its enduring legacy within the sports drama genre.

Chapter 7 - Eddie (1996)
Fictional Comedy Starring Whoopi Goldberg as a Coach

In the realm of sports films, where drama and inspiration often take center stage, "Eddie" provides a unique and refreshing take as a fictional comedy led by the incomparable Whoopi Goldberg. This section explores the distinctive qualities of "Eddie" as it ventures into the realm of sports through humor and the charismatic presence of Goldberg as the unconventional coach. Through scene analysis, interviews with the filmmakers, and insights into Goldberg's portrayal, we unravel the intentional choices that make "Eddie" a standout comedy in the sports movie genre.

Setting the Stage: Whoopi Goldberg as Eddie

The comedic genius of Whoopi Goldberg takes center stage in "Eddie" as she portrays Eddie Franklin, a passionate and spirited New York Knicks fan thrust into the unexpected role of head coach. This section explores how Goldberg's persona infuses the film with humor and heart, establishing a unique tone that sets "Eddie" apart from conventional sports comedies. Through scene analysis, discussions with the director, and insights from Goldberg herself, we delve into the intentional choices that make Eddie a memorable and unconventional sports movie character.

The section considers scenes that introduce Eddie Franklin and showcase Goldberg's comedic prowess, exploring how the film establishes her character's deep connection to the New York Knicks. It analyzes moments that highlight Eddie's infectious enthusiasm and her journey from a superfan to an unexpected coaching sensation. The chapter also reflects on the collaborative effort between Goldberg and the filmmakers to create a character that resonates with audiences. By examining Goldberg's portrayal of Eddie, the section provides readers with insights into how the film navigates the intersection of sports and comedy.

A Fish Out of Water Tale: Eddie's Unlikely Journey

"Eddie" presents a classic fish out of water tale, placing an everyday fan in the midst of the professional sports world. This section explores how the film leverages the comedic potential of Eddie's unlikely journey from the stands to the sidelines. Through scene analysis, interviews with the screenwriter, and insights from Goldberg, we unravel the intentional choices that contribute to the humor and charm of Eddie's fish out of water narrative.

The section considers scenes that depict Eddie's introduction to the inner workings of professional basketball, exploring the comedic situations that arise from her newfound role as head coach. It analyzes moments that showcase Eddie's unconventional coaching style and her interactions with the players and staff. The chapter also reflects on the collaborative effort between the filmmakers and Goldberg to ensure a balance between humor and authenticity in depicting Eddie's journey. By examining the fish out of water narrative, the section provides readers with insights into how "Eddie" embraces the comedic potential of placing an ordinary fan in an extraordinary position.

Team Dynamics: Comedy Amidst the Court Drama

While sports movies often delve into the drama of team dynamics, "Eddie" infuses this narrative element with comedy. This section explores how the film navigates the traditional tropes of team dynamics, adding a layer of humor to the interpersonal relationships among the players and coaching staff. Through scene analysis, interviews with the actors, and insights from the director, we delve into the intentional choices that make "Eddie" a unique blend of sports drama and comedy.

The section considers scenes that highlight the interactions between Eddie and the diverse cast of characters on the team, exploring the comedic situations that arise from her unorthodox coaching methods. It analyzes moments that showcase the players' reactions to Eddie's unconventional approach and the humor derived from the clash of personalities. The chapter also reflects on the collaborative effort between the filmmakers and the cast to strike a balance between the dramatic elements of team dynamics and the comedic tone of the film. By examining team dynamics with a comedic lens, the section provides readers with insights into how "Eddie" reimagines the traditional portrayal of relationships within a sports team.

Challenges and Triumphs: Eddie's Impact on the Team

As Eddie navigates the challenges of coaching a professional basketball team, the film interweaves moments of triumph and humor. This section explores how "Eddie" portrays the impact of an unconventional coach on the team, blending the comedic elements with moments of genuine inspiration. Through scene analysis, discussions with the screenwriter, and insights from Goldberg, we unravel the intentional choices that depict Eddie's journey from an unlikely leader to a transformative figure for the team.

The section considers scenes that showcase the challenges faced by Eddie and the players, exploring the comedic and dramatic elements that arise from their journey. It analyzes moments that highlight Eddie's unconventional coaching strategies and the team's response to her unique approach. The chapter also reflects on the collaborative effort between the filmmakers and Goldberg to ensure a nuanced portrayal of Eddie's impact on the team. By examining the challenges and triumphs within the narrative, the section provides readers with insights into how "Eddie" navigates the delicate balance between humor and genuine emotional moments.

A New Perspective on Sports: Eddie's Impact Beyond the Court

"Eddie" not only brings humor to the basketball court but also offers a new perspective on the broader impact of sports on individuals and communities. This section explores how the film transcends its comedic elements to deliver a message about the transformative power of sports and fandom. Through scene analysis, interviews with the director, and insights from Goldberg, we delve into the intentional choices that elevate "Eddie" beyond a conventional sports comedy.

The section considers scenes that showcase the community's response to Eddie's coaching, exploring the film's portrayal of the societal importance of sports. It analyzes moments that highlight the unity and inspiration derived from the team's journey, emphasizing the film's message about the unifying power of sports fandom. The chapter also reflects on the collaborative effort between the filmmakers and Goldberg to ensure a meaningful exploration of the impact of sports on individuals and communities. By examining Eddie's impact beyond the court, the section provides readers with insights into how "Eddie" offers a fresh perspective on the cultural significance of sports.

Whoopi Goldberg's Comic Mastery: Elevating the Comedy Genre

At the heart of "Eddie" is Whoopi Goldberg's unparalleled comedic talent, which elevates the film beyond the traditional boundaries of sports comedy. This section explores how Goldberg's comic mastery contributes to the humor and authenticity of "Eddie." Through scene analysis, discussions with the director, and insights from Goldberg herself, we unravel the intentional choices that make Goldberg's performance a key element in the film's success.

The section considers scenes that showcase Goldberg's comedic timing and improvisational skills, exploring how she brings authenticity and humor to the character of Eddie. It analyzes moments that highlight Goldberg's ability to infuse the film with both lighthearted humor and genuine emotional depth. The chapter also reflects on the collaborative effort between Goldberg and the filmmakers to ensure a seamless integration of comedy into the sports genre. By examining Goldberg's comic mastery, the section provides readers with insights into how her performance defines the comedic spirit of "Eddie."

The Legacy of Laughter: "Eddie" in the Comedy Canon

As we conclude our exploration of "Eddie" as a fictional comedy starring Whoopi Goldberg as a coach, the section reflects on the enduring legacy of laughter that the film has left in the comedy canon. It considers how "Eddie" has carved its niche by combining sports, humor, and Goldberg's unique comedic style. Through critical analysis, reflections on the film's impact, and insights into the lasting appeal of the comedy genre, we unravel the factors that make "Eddie" a timeless addition to the world of sports comedies.

The section reflects on how "Eddie" continues to resonate with audiences, celebrating its place in the comedy canon and its enduring popularity as a sports-themed comedy. It considers the film's contributions to the broader landscape of sports movies and its unique position in blending humor with the world of professional basketball. The chapter also reflects on the collaborative effort between Goldberg, the filmmakers, and the comedic elements that have contributed to the lasting legacy of laughter associated with "Eddie." By examining the legacy of laughter, the section provides readers with a final appreciation of how "Eddie" stands as a comedic gem in the intersection of sports and humor.

Fish Out of Water Tale of a NYC Fan Turned Coach

In the bustling heart of New York City, where the rhythm of life beats to the pulse of basketball, "Eddie" emerges as a cinematic celebration of the unexpected. In this chapter, we delve into the heart of the film's narrative—a fish out of water tale that transforms a die-hard New York Knicks fan into an unconventional coach. Through scene analysis, interviews with the filmmakers, and insights into the vibrant performance of Whoopi Goldberg as Eddie, we unravel the intentional choices that make this fish out of water narrative a captivating exploration of sports, fandom, and the transformative power of unexpected opportunities.

A Love Letter to the Knicks: Establishing Eddie's Fandom

The streets of New York City are synonymous with basketball, and in "Eddie," the city's heartbeat resonates with the cheers for the beloved New York Knicks. This section explores how the film establishes Eddie's deep-seated fandom for the Knicks, setting the stage for her unlikely journey from a passionate fan to an integral part of the team. Through scene analysis, discussions with the director, and insights from Goldberg, we unravel the intentional choices that create a heartfelt love letter to the Knicks within the fabric of the film.

The section considers scenes that showcase Eddie's infectious enthusiasm for the Knicks, exploring how the film captures the essence of sports fandom in the heart of New York. It analyzes moments that highlight Eddie's unique connection to the team, setting the foundation for her transformation from a dedicated spectator to an unexpected participant. The chapter also reflects on the collaborative effort between the filmmakers and Goldberg to ensure an authentic portrayal of Eddie's genuine love for the Knicks. By examining the establishment of Eddie's fandom, the section provides readers with insights into how "Eddie" immerses itself in the cultural identity of New York City and its basketball fervor.

From the Stands to the Sidelines: Eddie's Unexpected Ascent

The transformation from a fervent fan in the stands to the head coach on the sidelines is the core premise of "Eddie," and this section explores the narrative arc that propels Eddie into the heart of the action. Through scene analysis, interviews with the screenwriter, and insights from Goldberg, we unravel the intentional choices that drive Eddie's unexpected ascent and turn a fish out of water tale into a captivating sports comedy.

The section considers scenes that depict the moment Eddie is thrust into the spotlight, exploring the comedic and dramatic elements that arise from her unexpected appointment as head coach. It analyzes moments that showcase Eddie's initial disorientation and her gradual adaptation to the challenges of her newfound role. The chapter also reflects on the collaborative effort between the filmmakers and Goldberg to navigate the delicate balance between humor and authenticity in portraying Eddie's journey. By examining Eddie's unexpected ascent, the section provides readers with insights into how "Eddie" skillfully navigates the transition from sports enthusiast to a central figure in the basketball drama.

A Coach Unlike Any Other: Eddie's Unconventional Style

As Eddie takes her place on the sidelines, the film unfolds a coaching style unlike any other seen in the world of professional basketball. This section explores how "Eddie" infuses humor into the conventional realm of coaching, presenting a protagonist who challenges norms and approaches the game with a refreshing, unconventional style. Through scene analysis, discussions with the screenwriter, and insights from Goldberg, we delve into the intentional choices that define Eddie's coaching philosophy and make her an unconventional yet endearing figure.

The section considers scenes that showcase Eddie's interactions with the players and staff, exploring the comedic situations that arise from her unorthodox coaching methods. It analyzes moments that highlight Eddie's refusal to conform to traditional coaching norms and her determination to inject fun and authenticity into the game. The chapter also reflects on the collaborative effort between the filmmakers and Goldberg to strike a balance between humor and genuine emotional moments in depicting Eddie's coaching style. By examining Eddie's unconventional approach, the section provides readers with insights into how "Eddie" challenges the stereotypical image of a coach and adds a layer of humor to the coaching narrative.

Navigating the Professional Arena: Eddie Among the Basketball Elite

As a fish out of water in the professional basketball arena, Eddie faces the challenges of navigating the dynamics of the sport at the highest level. This section explores how the film portrays Eddie's interactions with the players, management, and the media, highlighting the comedic situations that arise from her unconventional presence in the professional basketball world. Through scene analysis, interviews with the filmmakers, and insights from Goldberg, we unravel the intentional choices that create a rich tapestry of humor and authenticity as Eddie finds her place among the basketball elite.

The section considers scenes that depict Eddie's encounters with the players, exploring the humor derived from their reactions to her unconventional coaching style. It analyzes moments that showcase Eddie's interactions with the management and media, highlighting the challenges she faces as an outsider in the professional sports arena. The chapter also reflects on the collaborative effort between the filmmakers and Goldberg to ensure a nuanced portrayal of Eddie's journey from a superfan to a central figure in the professional basketball landscape. By examining Eddie's navigation of the professional arena, the section provides readers with insights into how "Eddie" masterfully balances humor and authenticity in depicting the clash between the ordinary and the extraordinary in the world of professional sports.

Bonding with the Players: Eddie's Impact Beyond the Court

Amidst the laughter and chaos, "Eddie" weaves a narrative of genuine connection between the unconventional coach and the players. This section explores how the film portrays Eddie's impact beyond the court, emphasizing the moments of bonding and camaraderie that transcend the traditional coach-player relationship. Through scene analysis, discussions with the screenwriter, and insights from Goldberg, we unravel the intentional choices that depict Eddie's transformative influence on the players and add depth to the film's narrative.

The section considers scenes that showcase Eddie's interactions with the players off the court, exploring the humor and heartwarming moments that arise from their growing connection. It analyzes moments that highlight Eddie's ability to bridge the gap between the players and the fans, emphasizing the film's message about the unifying power of sports fandom. The chapter also reflects on the collaborative effort between the filmmakers and Goldberg to ensure a meaningful exploration of the impact of an unconventional coach on the players' lives. By examining Eddie's bonding with the players, the section provides readers with insights into how "Eddie" goes beyond the comedic elements to deliver a message about the transformative power of genuine connections in the world of professional sports.

The Cultural Tapestry of New York City: Eddie's Impact Beyond Basketball

Beyond the basketball court, "Eddie" explores the broader impact of sports and fandom on the cultural tapestry of New York City. This section delves into how the film transcends its fish out of water narrative to deliver a message about the societal importance of sports in urban communities. Through scene analysis, interviews with the director, and insights from Goldberg, we unravel the intentional choices that elevate "Eddie" beyond a conventional sports comedy, offering a unique perspective on the cultural significance of sports in urban landscapes.

The section considers scenes that showcase the community's response to Eddie's coaching, exploring the film's portrayal of the societal importance of sports in the fabric of New York City. It analyzes moments that highlight the unity and inspiration derived from the team's journey, emphasizing the film's message about the unifying power of sports fandom. The chapter also reflects on the collaborative effort between the filmmakers and Goldberg to ensure a meaningful exploration of the impact of sports on individuals and communities. By examining Eddie's impact beyond basketball, the section provides readers with insights into how "Eddie" offers a fresh perspective on the cultural significance of sports in urban settings.

Whoopi Goldberg's Unforgettable Performance: The Heart of Eddie's Fish Out of Water Tale

At the heart of "Eddie" lies the unforgettable performance of Whoopi Goldberg, whose portrayal of Eddie Franklin adds depth, humor, and authenticity to the film's fish out of water narrative. This section explores Goldberg's contribution to the film, delving into her nuanced performance that transforms Eddie from a New York Knicks superfan to an unconventional yet endearing coach. Through scene analysis, discussions with the director, and insights from Goldberg herself, we unravel the intentional choices that make Goldberg's performance the beating heart of "Eddie."

The section considers scenes that showcase Goldberg's comedic timing and improvisational skills, exploring how she brings authenticity and humor to the character of Eddie. It analyzes moments that highlight Goldberg's ability to infuse the film with both lighthearted humor and genuine emotional depth. The chapter also reflects on the collaborative effort between Goldberg and the filmmakers to ensure a seamless integration of comedy into the sports genre. By examining Goldberg's unforgettable performance, the section provides readers with insights into how her portrayal defines the comedic spirit and emotional resonance of "Eddie."

The Enduring Legacy of a Fish Out of Water Tale: "Eddie" in Film History

As we conclude our exploration of "Eddie" as a fish out of water tale of a New York City fan turned coach, the section reflects on the enduring legacy of the film within the broader landscape of cinema. It considers how "Eddie" has carved its niche by combining sports, humor, and Goldberg's unique performance. Through critical analysis, reflections on the film's impact, and insights into the lasting appeal of fish out of water narratives, we unravel the factors that make "Eddie" a timeless addition to the world of sports comedies.

The section reflects on how "Eddie" continues to resonate with audiences, celebrating its place in film history as a fish out of water tale that defies conventions. It considers the film's contributions to the broader landscape of sports movies and its unique position in blending humor with the world of professional basketball. The chapter also reflects on the collaborative effort between Goldberg, the filmmakers, and the comedic elements that have contributed to the lasting legacy of "Eddie." By examining the enduring legacy of a fish out of water tale, the section provides readers with a final appreciation of how "Eddie" stands as a comedic gem in the intersection of sports and humor within film history.

Another Underdog Team Overcoming Odds

In the rich tapestry of sports cinema, the underdog narrative is a thread that weaves its way through the heart of compelling stories. In "Eddie," the concept of the underdog takes center stage as a group of unlikely players, guided by the unorthodox coaching style of Whoopi Goldberg's Eddie Franklin, strives to overcome the odds and leave an indelible mark on the basketball court. This chapter delves into the intricacies of the underdog theme within the film, exploring how "Eddie" transforms a disparate group of players into a cohesive team on a journey of self-discovery, triumph, and laughter.

Establishing the Underdog Narrative: Eddie's Transformational Role

"Eddie" unfolds as a quintessential underdog story, with the New York Knicks portrayed as a struggling team in dire need of a turnaround. This section explores the film's establishment of the underdog narrative and how Eddie's unconventional coaching methods serve as a catalyst for the team's transformation. Through scene analysis, discussions with the screenwriter, and insights from Goldberg, we unravel the intentional choices that position Eddie as the catalyst for change within the underdog narrative.

The section considers scenes that depict the struggling state of the New York Knicks at the outset, exploring the challenges faced by the team and its players. It analyzes moments that showcase Eddie's introduction to the team, emphasizing how her unconventional coaching style becomes the driving force behind the underdog narrative. The chapter also reflects on the collaborative effort between the filmmakers and Goldberg to ensure a seamless integration of the underdog theme into the broader narrative. By examining the establishment of the underdog narrative, the section provides readers with insights into how "Eddie" sets the stage for a transformative journey of overcoming odds.

A Diverse Cast of Characters: Players Embracing Their Underdog Status

As Eddie takes charge of the New York Knicks, the film introduces a diverse cast of characters, each grappling with their own challenges and embodying the underdog spirit. This section explores how "Eddie" carefully crafts the individual narratives of the players, showcasing their unique struggles and aspirations. Through scene analysis, interviews with the actors, and insights from the director, we unravel the intentional choices that contribute to the authenticity and depth of the characters as they navigate their underdog status.

The section considers scenes that highlight the diverse backgrounds and personalities of the players, exploring how their individual journeys contribute to the overarching underdog narrative. It analyzes moments that showcase the players embracing their underdog status, emphasizing their determination to rise above challenges and prove themselves on the court. The chapter also reflects on the collaborative effort between the filmmakers and the cast to ensure nuanced portrayals of the characters' underdog journeys. By examining the diverse cast of characters, the section provides readers with insights into how "Eddie" humanizes the underdog narrative, making it a story of individual triumphs within the broader team dynamic.

Humor Amidst Hardships: Eddie's Comedic Approach to Coaching

In the realm of sports comedies, "Eddie" stands out for its ability to infuse humor into the underdog narrative. This section explores how the film employs Eddie's comedic coaching style to bring levity to the challenges faced by the underdog team. Through scene analysis, discussions with the screenwriter, and insights from Goldberg, we unravel the intentional choices that use humor as a tool for resilience and camaraderie within the underdog journey.

The section considers scenes that depict Eddie's unconventional coaching methods, exploring how humor becomes a coping mechanism for the players as they navigate their underdog status. It analyzes moments that showcase Eddie's ability to use laughter as a unifying force, emphasizing how humor becomes a thread that binds the team together. The chapter also reflects on the collaborative effort between the filmmakers and Goldberg to strike a balance between the comedic elements and the genuine emotional resonance of the underdog narrative. By examining humor amidst hardships, the section provides readers with insights into how "Eddie" redefines the traditional underdog story by infusing it with laughter and camaraderie.

Challenges on and off the Court: Overcoming Adversity

The underdog journey is never without its share of challenges, both on and off the basketball court. This section explores how "Eddie" portrays the team's struggles and triumphs, emphasizing the resilience required to overcome adversity. Through scene analysis, interviews with the filmmakers, and insights from Goldberg, we unravel the intentional choices that create a dynamic narrative of overcoming challenges within the broader underdog theme.

The section considers scenes that depict the team facing adversity on the court, exploring the challenges they encounter during games and competitions. It analyzes moments that showcase the players confronting personal obstacles off the court, emphasizing the interconnectedness of their individual struggles with the broader underdog narrative. The chapter also reflects on the collaborative effort between the filmmakers and Goldberg to ensure a realistic portrayal of the challenges faced by the team. By examining challenges on and off the court, the section provides readers with insights into how "Eddie" elevates the underdog narrative by presenting a multifaceted journey of triumph over adversity.

Unity in Diversity: The Team Forging a Collective Identity

As the underdog team navigates the trials and tribulations of their journey, "Eddie" emphasizes the importance of unity in diversity. This section explores how the film portrays the team forging a collective identity, transcending individual differences to become a cohesive unit. Through scene analysis, discussions with the screenwriter, and insights from Goldberg, we unravel the intentional choices that highlight the transformative power of teamwork within the underdog narrative.

The section considers scenes that showcase the players coming together as a team, exploring the moments of unity that define their collective identity. It analyzes how the film navigates the diverse backgrounds and personalities of the players, emphasizing the strength derived from their shared underdog status. The chapter also reflects on the collaborative effort between the filmmakers and Goldberg to ensure a nuanced portrayal of the team's journey toward unity. By examining the unity in diversity, the section provides readers with insights into how "Eddie" elevates the underdog narrative by celebrating the transformative potential of collective identity.

Triumph on the Court: Underdog Success and Its Impact

In the grand tradition of underdog stories, "Eddie" builds towards a climactic moment of triumph on the basketball court. This section explores how the film portrays the underdog team's success and the impact of their triumph on the broader narrative. Through scene analysis, interviews with the filmmakers, and insights from Goldberg, we unravel the intentional choices that create a sense of fulfillment and celebration within the underdog journey.

The section considers scenes that depict the team's success on the court, exploring the emotional and narrative impact of their underdog triumph. It analyzes moments that showcase the reactions of the players, fans, and the broader community, emphasizing the far-reaching consequences of the team's success. The chapter also reflects on the collaborative effort between the filmmakers and Goldberg to ensure a satisfying and authentic portrayal of the underdog team's triumph. By examining triumph on the court, the section provides readers with insights into how "Eddie" delivers a cathartic and uplifting conclusion to the underdog narrative.

Legacy Beyond the Game: The Underdog Theme in Film History

As we conclude our exploration of "Eddie" as another underdog team overcoming odds, this section reflects on the enduring legacy of the underdog theme within the broader landscape of cinema. It considers how "Eddie" contributes to the rich tradition of underdog narratives in sports movies, celebrating its place as a film that transcends conventions. Through critical analysis, reflections on the film's impact, and insights into the lasting appeal of the underdog theme, we unravel the factors that make "Eddie" a timeless addition to the world of sports comedies.

The section reflects on how "Eddie" continues to resonate with audiences, celebrating its place in film history as a compelling underdog story that defies conventions. It considers the film's contributions to the broader landscape of sports movies and its unique position in blending humor with the world of professional basketball. The chapter also reflects on the collaborative effort between the filmmakers, the cast, and the underdog theme that has contributed to the lasting legacy of "Eddie." By examining the enduring legacy of another underdog team overcoming odds, the section provides readers with a final appreciation of how "Eddie" stands as a timeless underdog tale within the annals of film history.

One of Several '90s Films Focused on Coaches

In the realm of '90s cinema, a distinct trend emerged—a fascination with the role of coaches and their transformative impact on teams, athletes, and even themselves. "Eddie," a unique entry in this trend, takes the spotlight as a sports comedy that not only places a coach at its narrative core but does so with a comedic twist. This chapter explores the broader cinematic landscape of '90s coach-focused films, contextualizing "Eddie" within this thematic framework. Through an analysis of key films, interviews with filmmakers, and insights from cultural critics, we unravel the intentional choices that position "Eddie" as one among several '90s films that delves into the complex and often comedic world of coaching.

The Coach-Centric Trend in '90s Cinema: A Cultural Snapshot

The 1990s witnessed a cinematic preoccupation with the figure of the coach—a central and often charismatic character whose influence extended far beyond the boundaries of the playing field. This section delves into the cultural backdrop that fueled the popularity of coach-centric narratives during this era. Through an exploration of societal shifts, evolving perceptions of sports, and the broader landscape of '90s cinema, we unravel the factors that contributed to the emergence of coaches as compelling protagonists in storytelling.

The section considers the socio-cultural factors that shaped the narrative landscape of the 1990s, exploring how societal values and attitudes toward sports and mentorship influenced the thematic choices of filmmakers. It analyzes the evolving depiction of coaches in popular media during this era, emphasizing the transition from coaches as peripheral figures to central characters driving the narrative. The chapter also reflects on how the '90s coach-centric trend tapped into broader themes of leadership, mentorship, and personal growth, resonating with audiences seeking stories that extended beyond the confines of traditional sports dramas. By examining the coach-centric trend in '90s cinema, the section provides readers with insights into the cultural snapshot that set the stage for films like "Eddie."

Eddie and the Comedy of Coaching: A Unique Take on a Familiar Theme

While '90s cinema embraced coach-centric narratives, "Eddie" distinguished itself by infusing humor into the traditional coaching story. This section explores how "Eddie" adopts a comedic lens to depict the world of coaching, offering a fresh and entertaining perspective on the familiar theme. Through scene analysis, discussions with the screenwriter, and insights from Goldberg, we unravel the intentional choices that position "Eddie" as a standout entry in the coach-centric trend, balancing humor with genuine emotional depth.

The section considers scenes that showcase Eddie's comedic coaching style, exploring how the film uses humor as a vehicle for both satire and genuine insight into coaching dynamics. It analyzes moments that highlight the film's unique approach to blending comedy with the challenges and triumphs of coaching, emphasizing the distinctiveness of "Eddie" within the broader coach-centric trend. The chapter also reflects on the collaborative effort between the filmmakers and Goldberg to strike a balance between humor and authenticity, ensuring that "Eddie" offers a comedic take on coaching without sacrificing the emotional resonance of the narrative. By examining the comedy of coaching in "Eddie," the section provides readers with insights into how the film navigates the fine line between satire and homage within the coach-centric theme.

Eddie vs. the Coaching Stereotype: Deconstructing Tropes

As "Eddie" positions itself within the coach-centric trend, the film actively engages with and deconstructs coaching stereotypes prevalent in '90s cinema. This section explores how the film challenges conventional perceptions of coaches, offering a nuanced and at times irreverent take on the archetype. Through scene analysis, discussions with the screenwriter, and insights from Goldberg, we unravel the intentional choices that distinguish Eddie's character from traditional coaching tropes, adding depth and complexity to the narrative.

The section considers scenes that depict Eddie's interactions with coaching stereotypes, exploring how the film confronts and subverts expectations surrounding the figure of the coach. It analyzes moments that showcase Eddie's refusal to conform to conventional coaching norms, emphasizing the film's commitment to presenting a character who defies stereotypes. The chapter also reflects on the collaborative effort between the filmmakers and Goldberg to ensure a subversive yet respectful portrayal of coaching stereotypes, allowing

"Eddie" to simultaneously challenge and embrace the conventions of coach-centric narratives. By examining Eddie's confrontation with coaching stereotypes, the section provides readers with insights into how "Eddie" adds a layer of complexity to the coach-centric theme by deconstructing familiar tropes.

The '90s Coach Film Pantheon: Eddie in Good Company

As "Eddie" joins the ranks of coach-centric films from the 1990s, this section provides a curated exploration of key films that shaped the cinematic landscape of the era. Through an analysis of iconic coach-focused movies, interviews with filmmakers, and insights from cultural critics, we unravel the thematic threads that connect "Eddie" to its '90s counterparts. The section considers the unique qualities of each film, exploring how they contributed to the diverse and evolving narrative of coaches in cinema during this vibrant decade.

The section examines films such as "Remember the Titans," "The Mighty Ducks," and "A League of Their Own," among others, to draw connections between their thematic choices and the narrative landscape of "Eddie." It analyzes how each film approached the coach-centric theme, emphasizing the distinctive qualities that set them apart within the broader cinematic panorama. The chapter also reflects on the collective impact of these films on shaping audience expectations and cultural perceptions of coaches during the '90s. By exploring the '90s coach film pantheon, the section provides readers with a comprehensive view of how "Eddie" becomes part of a dynamic conversation within a cinematic era defined by its fascination with coaching narratives.

Coach-Centric Narratives Beyond the '90s: A Cinematic Legacy

As we conclude our exploration of "Eddie" within the context of the '90s coach-centric trend, this section reflects on the enduring legacy of coach-focused narratives in cinema beyond the turn of the millennium. It considers how the thematic choices and storytelling innovations of '90s films, including "Eddie," continue to influence contemporary portrayals of coaches on the big screen. Through critical analysis, reflections on the evolving role of coaches in sports cinema, and insights into the lasting appeal of coach-centric narratives, we unravel the factors that contribute to the enduring cinematic legacy of coaching stories.

The section reflects on how "Eddie" has left its mark on the ongoing conversation about coaches in cinema, celebrating its place in film history as a unique and memorable entry in the coach-centric genre. It considers the film's contributions to the broader landscape of sports movies and its influence on contemporary portrayals of coaches in both comedic and dramatic narratives. The chapter also reflects on the collaborative effort between the filmmakers, the cast, and the coach-centric trend that has contributed to the lasting legacy of "Eddie" and similar films. By examining the cinematic legacy of coach-centric narratives beyond the '90s, the section provides readers with a final appreciation of how "Eddie" continues to resonate as a comedic gem within the annals of sports cinema.

Chapter 8 - Glory Road (2006)
Chronicling Texas Western's Barrier-Breaking Title

In the annals of college basketball history, certain moments transcend the game itself, leaving an indelible mark on the collective consciousness. "Glory Road" takes its place as a cinematic tribute to one such transformative moment—the historic victory of the Texas Western Miners in the 1966 NCAA Championship. This chapter delves into the film's portrayal of the barrier-breaking title run, exploring how "Glory Road" captures the essence of a team that defied convention, shattered racial barriers, and etched its name in the chronicles of basketball history.

Setting the Stage: Basketball and Society in the 1960s

Before delving into the narrative intricacies of "Glory Road," this section provides a historical backdrop to the sociopolitical landscape of the 1960s. The turbulent era, marked by civil rights struggles and changing cultural dynamics, significantly influenced the world of college basketball. Through an examination of key events, interviews with historians, and insights from the filmmakers, we unravel the intersections between basketball and society, setting the stage for the remarkable journey of the Texas Western Miners.

The section considers how the civil rights movement and shifting attitudes toward racial integration impacted college sports, particularly basketball, during the 1960s. It analyzes the cultural significance of basketball as a stage for social change, emphasizing its role in challenging entrenched racial norms. The chapter also reflects on the collaborative effort between the filmmakers and historical consultants to ensure an authentic portrayal of the era's socio-political climate. By examining the setting of the stage in "Glory Road," the section provides readers with insights into the contextual elements that shaped the narrative of Texas Western's barrier-breaking title.

Texas Western's Journey: From Underdogs to Champions

At the heart of "Glory Road" is the compelling narrative of the Texas Western Miners—a team that, against all odds, emerged as champions. This section explores the film's portrayal of the team's journey, from its humble beginnings to the pinnacle of college basketball success. Through scene analysis, discussions with the screenwriter, and insights from historical consultants, we unravel the intentional choices that bring to life the underdog story of Texas Western.

The section considers scenes that depict the team's early struggles and the formation of a roster that would go on to make history. It analyzes moments that showcase the dynamics between the players, the coaching staff, and the challenges they faced both on and off the court. The chapter also reflects on the collaborative effort between the filmmakers and former players to ensure an authentic portrayal of the team's journey, capturing the spirit of resilience, camaraderie, and determination that defined Texas Western's path to the championship. By examining Texas Western's journey in "Glory Road," the section provides readers with insights into the narrative elements that transform a basketball team into a symbol of courage and accomplishment.

Don Haskins: Coaching the Unconventional

A central figure in the Texas Western narrative is Coach Don Haskins—an unconventional leader who challenged the status quo of college basketball. This section explores the film's portrayal of Haskins and his coaching philosophy, examining how "Glory Road" presents a nuanced and at times controversial depiction of a coach who left an indelible mark on the sport. Through scene analysis, discussions with the screenwriter, and insights from those who knew Haskins, we unravel the intentional choices that shape the character of the coach who guided Texas Western to glory.

The section considers scenes that depict Haskins' unconventional coaching methods, exploring the moments that define his approach to the game and his interactions with players. It analyzes the film's portrayal of Haskins' challenges within the broader basketball community, emphasizing the complexities of coaching during an era marked by racial tensions. The chapter also reflects on the collaborative effort between the filmmakers and individuals close to Haskins to ensure a respectful yet critical portrayal of the coach's legacy. By examining Don Haskins' coaching style in "Glory Road," the section provides readers with insights into the film's exploration of leadership, innovation, and the impact of an unorthodox coaching philosophy on the court and beyond.

Shattering Racial Barriers: The Texas Western Starting Five

One of the defining aspects of Texas Western's championship run was its starting lineup—a lineup that would make history by being the first all-black starting five in an NCAA championship game. This section explores the film's portrayal of the racial dynamics within the team, examining the significance of the starting five in the context of the civil rights movement and the broader struggle for racial equality. Through scene analysis, interviews with the cast, and insights from historical consultants, we unravel the intentional choices that capture the racial dynamics of the Texas Western team.

The section considers scenes that depict the challenges faced by the black players on the team, exploring the racial tensions within the broader basketball community and the larger society. It analyzes the film's portrayal of the relationships between the black and white players, emphasizing the camaraderie that developed amidst societal prejudices. The chapter also reflects on the collaborative effort between the filmmakers and former players to ensure an authentic portrayal of the racial dynamics within the team, capturing the courage and resilience of those who shattered racial barriers on the court. By examining the racial dynamics of the Texas Western team in "Glory Road," the section provides readers with insights into the film's exploration of racial equality, unity, and the transformative power of sports in challenging societal norms.

The Championship Game: A Triumph Beyond the Scoreboard

At the heart of "Glory Road" lies the climactic championship game—a contest that goes beyond the scoreboard, symbolizing a triumph of perseverance, courage, and social change. This section explores the film's portrayal of the championship game, examining how it captures the intensity of the on-court battle and the broader cultural significance of Texas Western's victory. Through scene analysis, interviews with the filmmakers, and insights from those who were there, we unravel the intentional choices that elevate the championship game to a pivotal moment in the history of college basketball.

The section considers scenes that depict the drama of the championship game, exploring the emotional highs and lows experienced by the players and the stakes involved in the historical matchup. It analyzes the film's portrayal of the broader impact of Texas Western's victory on the landscape of college sports, emphasizing the cultural resonance of the team's triumph. The chapter also reflects on the collaborative effort between the filmmakers and historical consultants to ensure an accurate and evocative portrayal of the championship game, capturing the essence of a moment that transcended basketball. By examining the championship game in "Glory Road," the section provides readers with insights into the film's exploration of victory, legacy, and the enduring impact of a barrier-breaking triumph.

Legacy of Glory: Texas Western's Enduring Impact

As we conclude our exploration of "Glory Road" and its chronicling of Texas Western's barrier-breaking title, this section reflects on the enduring legacy of the team's historic victory. It considers how the film contributes to the broader cultural understanding of Texas Western's impact on college basketball, civil rights, and the ongoing quest for equality. Through critical analysis, reflections on the film's cultural significance, and insights into the lasting appeal of Texas Western's story, we unravel the factors that make "Glory Road" a timeless tribute to a team that changed the game and challenged the status quo.

The section reflects on how "Glory Road" continues to resonate with audiences, celebrating its place in film history as a compelling portrayal of a transformative moment in sports. It considers the film's contributions to the broader landscape of sports movies and its unique position in capturing the cultural and historical significance of Texas Western's championship. The chapter also reflects on the collaborative effort between the filmmakers, the cast, and historical consultants that has contributed to the lasting legacy of "Glory Road." By examining the enduring impact of Texas Western's barrier-breaking title, the section provides readers with a final appreciation of how "Glory Road" stands as a timeless tribute to a team that transcended the court and left an indelible mark on the history of college basketball.

Josh Lucas as Pioneering Coach Don Haskins

In the portrayal of historical figures on the big screen, casting becomes a pivotal element in capturing the essence of their characters. In "Glory Road," the transformative role of Coach Don Haskins is brought to life by actor Josh Lucas. This section delves into Lucas's portrayal of the pioneering coach, examining how his performance contributes to the film's narrative, explores the nuances of Haskins's character, and adds depth to the broader themes of basketball, race, and societal change.

Casting Don Haskins: The Crucial Decision

Before delving into Josh Lucas's portrayal, this section provides insights into the casting process and the significance of selecting an actor to embody the legendary Coach Don Haskins. Through interviews with the casting director, discussions with the filmmakers, and reflections from Josh Lucas himself, we unravel the considerations that went into choosing the actor tasked with bringing Haskins to life on the screen.

The section explores the criteria for casting the pivotal role of Coach Haskins, considering the physical attributes, acting prowess, and the ability to convey the complexities of the character. It delves into the challenges and responsibilities that come with portraying a real-life figure, especially one as iconic and influential as Haskins. The chapter also reflects on the collaborative efforts between the casting team, filmmakers, and historical consultants to ensure an authentic and respectful portrayal of the pioneering coach. By examining the casting of Coach Haskins, the section provides readers with insights into the careful considerations that precede bringing historical figures to life in cinematic narratives.

Josh Lucas: Embodying Don Haskins

Josh Lucas steps into the shoes of Coach Don Haskins, undertaking the formidable task of portraying a coach whose legacy looms large in the history of college basketball. This section delves into Lucas's performance, exploring how he captures the essence of Haskins's personality, coaching style, and the unique challenges he faced during the historic 1965-66 season. Through scene analysis, interviews with the actor, and insights from historical consultants, we unravel the intentional choices that define Lucas's portrayal of the pioneering coach.

The section considers scenes that showcase Lucas's embodiment of Haskins's on-court persona, exploring the nuances of the coach's interactions with players, peers, and the broader basketball community. It analyzes the film's portrayal of Haskins's emotional journey throughout the season, emphasizing the moments that highlight the complexities of his character. The chapter also reflects on the collaborative effort between Lucas, the filmmakers, and individuals who knew Haskins to ensure an accurate and evocative portrayal of the pioneering coach. By examining Josh Lucas's performance as Coach Haskins, the section provides readers with insights into the actor's approach to capturing the spirit of a coach whose impact transcended the game.

Capturing Haskins's Coaching Style: A Balance of Toughness and Empathy

At the core of Haskins's coaching philosophy was a unique blend of toughness and empathy—a balance that set him apart in the world of college basketball. This section explores how Josh Lucas captures the essence of Haskins's coaching style, examining the moments in the film that depict the coach's interactions with players, his strategic decisions, and the challenges he faced in navigating racial dynamics within the team.

The section considers scenes that highlight Haskins's tough love approach, exploring the moments that showcase his discipline, high expectations, and unwavering commitment to excellence. It analyzes the film's portrayal of Haskins's interactions with players from diverse backgrounds, emphasizing the coach's ability to foster a sense of unity amidst societal tensions. The chapter also reflects on the collaborative effort between Lucas, the filmmakers, and former players to ensure an authentic representation of Haskins's coaching style, capturing the complexities of leadership in a challenging historical context. By examining the portrayal of Haskins's coaching style, the section provides readers with insights into how Josh Lucas navigates the delicate balance of toughness and empathy that defined the legendary coach.

Emotional Depth: Haskins's Personal Journey

Beyond the basketball court, "Glory Road" delves into the personal journey of Coach Haskins—an aspect of the narrative that adds emotional depth to the character. This section explores how Josh Lucas conveys the emotional nuances of Haskins's journey, from the challenges he faced as a coach to the impact of societal expectations and his evolving relationships with the players.

The section considers scenes that depict Haskins's moments of introspection, exploring the emotional weight of his decisions and the toll that pioneering change in the face of adversity takes on the coach. It analyzes the film's portrayal of Haskins's relationships with his family, colleagues, and the players, emphasizing the human side of a figure often viewed through the lens of sports history. The chapter also reflects on the collaborative effort between Lucas, the filmmakers, and those who knew Haskins intimately to ensure a portrayal that goes beyond the surface and captures the emotional complexity of the coach's personal journey. By examining the emotional depth of Haskins's character, the section provides readers with insights into how Josh Lucas infuses the portrayal with authenticity and empathy, creating a multidimensional depiction of the pioneering coach.

Navigating Racial Dynamics: Haskins and the Integration of Texas Western

One of the central themes of "Glory Road" is the racial integration of the Texas Western basketball team, a pivotal moment in the history of college sports. This section explores how Josh Lucas navigates the racial dynamics of the narrative, examining the film's portrayal of Haskins's role in fostering unity among a racially diverse group of players during a tumultuous era.

The section considers scenes that depict Haskins's commitment to equality and meritocracy, exploring the moments that highlight his resistance to racial bias and his insistence on selecting players based on skill rather than race. It analyzes the film's portrayal of Haskins's interactions with players, addressing racial tensions within the team and the broader basketball community. The chapter also reflects on the collaborative effort between Lucas, the filmmakers, and former players to ensure an authentic representation of Haskins's stance on racial integration, capturing the coach's pivotal role in challenging norms and fostering a groundbreaking moment in sports history. By examining Josh Lucas's portrayal of Haskins's role in navigating racial dynamics, the section provides readers with insights into the actor's approach to capturing the coach's impact on the integration of Texas Western.

The Legacy of Josh Lucas's Haskins: A Cinematic Tribute

As we conclude our exploration of Josh Lucas's portrayal of Coach Don Haskins in "Glory Road," this section reflects on the enduring legacy of the actor's performance. It considers how Lucas's portrayal contributes to the broader cultural understanding of Haskins's impact on college basketball, civil rights, and the ongoing quest for equality. Through critical analysis, reflections on the cultural significance of the portrayal, and insights into the lasting appeal of Lucas's Haskins, we unravel the factors that make the performance a timeless tribute to a coach who changed the game and challenged the status quo.

The section reflects on how Lucas's portrayal continues to resonate with audiences, celebrating its place in film history as a compelling depiction of a transformative coach. It considers the performance's contributions to the broader landscape of sports movies and its unique position in capturing the cultural and historical significance of Coach Haskins. The chapter also reflects on the collaborative effort between Lucas, the filmmakers, and historical consultants that has contributed to the lasting legacy of the portrayal. By examining the enduring impact of Josh Lucas's Haskins, the section provides readers with a final appreciation of how the actor's performance stands as a timeless tribute to a coach whose influence transcended the court and left an indelible mark on the history of college basketball.

Examining the Racial Tensions of College Hoops in the '60s

The 1960s were a time of profound societal change in the United States, and college basketball was not immune to the seismic shifts occurring across the nation. "Glory Road" masterfully captures the racial tensions that permeated college hoops during this era, presenting a poignant narrative that goes beyond the game. This section delves into the film's exploration of the racial dynamics of college basketball in the '60s, examining how "Glory Road" navigates the challenges, prejudices, and transformative moments that defined this tumultuous period.

The Landscape of College Basketball in the '60s: A Divided Court

Before exploring the narrative intricacies of "Glory Road," this section provides historical context to the racial landscape of college basketball in the 1960s. It considers the broader societal changes that influenced the sport, examining the racial divisions within teams, conferences, and the NCAA. Through interviews with historians, insights from the filmmakers, and reflections on the state of college basketball in the '60s, we unravel the complexities of a divided court and the challenges faced by black players aspiring to compete at the highest levels.

The section delves into the racial dynamics within college basketball, exploring the limitations placed on black players in terms of scholarships, recruitment, and opportunities to showcase their talent. It analyzes the societal attitudes that perpetuated racial segregation within the sport and the resistance faced by black athletes challenging the status quo. The chapter also reflects on the collaborative effort between the filmmakers and historical consultants to ensure an authentic portrayal of the racial tensions that defined college basketball in the '60s. By examining the landscape of college basketball during this tumultuous period, the section provides readers with insights into the societal and institutional barriers that shaped the narrative of "Glory Road."

Texas Western's Pioneering Integration: Breaking Barriers

"Glory Road" centers around the Texas Western Miners' groundbreaking decision to field the first all-black starting lineup in an NCAA championship game. This section explores the film's portrayal of the team's journey towards integration, examining the challenges faced by Coach Don Haskins and the players as they sought to break down racial barriers and challenge the deeply ingrained prejudices within the world of college basketball.

The section considers scenes that depict the strategic decisions made by Haskins to field an all-black starting lineup, exploring the reactions from both within and outside the team. It analyzes the film's portrayal of the racial tensions that emerged within the team, highlighting the resistance faced by black players as they sought equal footing on the court. The chapter also reflects on the collaborative effort between the filmmakers, historical consultants, and former players to ensure an authentic representation of the pioneering integration efforts of Texas Western. By examining Texas Western's journey toward integration, the section provides readers with insights into the courage, determination, and sacrifices required to challenge racial norms within the realm of college basketball.

Player Perspectives: Navigating Prejudice and Paving the Way

"Glory Road" not only captures the broader racial dynamics of college basketball but also delves into the personal experiences of the black players who were at the forefront of the integration movement. This section explores the film's portrayal of the players' perspectives, examining their individual journeys, the prejudices they faced, and the impact of their pioneering efforts on the trajectory of college hoops.

The section considers scenes that depict the challenges faced by individual players, exploring their interactions with teammates, opponents, and the broader basketball community. It analyzes the film's portrayal of the players' resilience in the face of racial prejudices, emphasizing the camaraderie that developed within the team as they navigated a landscape resistant to change. The chapter also reflects on the collaborative effort between the filmmakers and former players to ensure an authentic representation of the personal struggles and triumphs of those who paved the way for future generations. By examining the player perspectives in "Glory Road," the section provides readers with insights into the emotional, psychological, and social dimensions of breaking racial barriers in college basketball.

Coach Haskins's Battle: Confronting Bias and Navigating Change

At the heart of "Glory Road" is Coach Don Haskins's battle against racial biases and his commitment to fostering an inclusive team. This section explores the film's portrayal of Haskins's role in confronting institutional prejudices, challenging societal norms, and navigating the complexities of integrating a racially diverse team.

The section considers scenes that depict Haskins's strategic decisions, confrontations with opposing coaches, and resistance from within the basketball community. It analyzes the film's portrayal of Haskins's unwavering commitment to meritocracy, emphasizing his determination to select players based on skill rather than race. The chapter also reflects on the collaborative effort between the filmmakers and historical consultants to ensure an authentic representation of Haskins's battle against bias, capturing the coach's pivotal role in driving change within college basketball. By examining Coach Haskins's battle in "Glory Road," the section provides readers with insights into the leadership, courage, and resilience required to confront racial prejudices within the realm of sports.

The Triumph of Texas Western: Beyond the Scoreboard

The climactic championship game in "Glory Road" represents more than a triumph on the basketball court—it symbolizes the triumph over racial barriers that defined the era. This section explores the film's portrayal of the championship game, examining how the victory of Texas Western went beyond the scoreboard and reverberated through the broader cultural and social fabric of the United States.

The section considers scenes that depict the emotional highs and lows of the championship game, exploring the broader impact of Texas Western's victory on the landscape of college sports. It analyzes the film's portrayal of the cultural resonance of the team's triumph, emphasizing the transformative power of sports in challenging societal norms. The chapter also reflects on the collaborative effort between the filmmakers and historical consultants to ensure an accurate and evocative representation of the cultural significance of Texas Western's victory. By examining the triumph of Texas Western in "Glory Road," the section provides readers with insights into how sports can serve as a catalyst for social change, breaking down racial barriers and inspiring a nation to reconsider deeply ingrained prejudices.

Legacy and Reflection: "Glory Road" and the Ongoing Pursuit of Equality

As we conclude our exploration of "Glory Road" and its examination of the racial tensions of college hoops in the '60s, this section reflects on the enduring legacy of the film. It considers how "Glory Road" contributes to the broader cultural understanding of the struggles and triumphs of those who challenged racial norms within the world of college basketball. Through critical analysis, reflections on the cultural significance of the film, and insights into the lasting impact of its portrayal of racial tensions, we unravel the factors that make "Glory Road" a timeless tribute to the pioneers who navigated a divided court and paved the way for a more inclusive future.

The section reflects on how "Glory Road" continues to resonate with audiences, celebrating its place in film history as a compelling depiction of a transformative moment in sports. It considers the film's contributions to the broader landscape of sports movies and its unique position in capturing the cultural and historical significance of Texas Western's triumph. The chapter also reflects on the collaborative effort between the filmmakers, historical consultants, and former players that has contributed to the lasting legacy of "Glory Road." By examining the enduring impact of the film's portrayal of racial tensions in college hoops, the section provides readers with a final appreciation of how "Glory Road" stands as a cinematic testament to the resilience, courage, and transformative power of those who challenged racial norms within the realm of college basketball in the '60s.

Taking Some Dramatic License With Events and Timelines

While "Glory Road" stands as a powerful cinematic portrayal of the Texas Western Miners' historic championship run, it is essential to acknowledge that the film, like many based on true events, takes certain liberties with the timeline and events for dramatic effect. This section delves into the creative choices made by the filmmakers, examining where "Glory Road" deviates from historical accuracy, and how these departures contribute to the film's narrative impact, emotional resonance, and broader themes.

The Art of Adaptation: Balancing Fact and Fiction

Before delving into the specific instances of dramatic license in "Glory Road," this section explores the broader concept of adaptation and the challenges inherent in translating real events into a compelling cinematic narrative. Through interviews with the filmmakers, discussions with historians, and insights into the creative process, we unravel the considerations that go into balancing historical accuracy with the demands of storytelling.

The section delves into the complexities of adapting real-life events for the screen, considering the inherent challenges of compressing timelines, consolidating characters, and enhancing dramatic tension. It analyzes the filmmakers' approach to balancing the need for authenticity with the artistic license required to craft a compelling narrative. The chapter also reflects on the collaborative effort between the filmmakers and historical consultants, acknowledging the delicate dance between preserving the essence of the true story and creating a cinematic experience that resonates with audiences. By examining the art of adaptation, the section provides readers with insights into the creative choices and challenges that shape the intersection of history and cinema.

Timeline Compression: Streamlining for Cinematic Impact

One of the common practices in adapting historical events for film is the compression of timelines to create a more streamlined and engaging narrative. This section explores how "Glory Road" employs timeline compression, condensing events and sequences to maintain a brisk pace and heighten the emotional impact of the story.

The section considers specific instances where the film condenses events, exploring the implications of such creative choices on the overall narrative flow. It analyzes the impact of timeline compression on character development, storytelling efficiency, and the emotional resonance of key moments. The chapter also reflects on the collaborative effort between the filmmakers and historical consultants to ensure that, despite the compressed timeline, the film retains the essential truths and themes of the Texas Western story. By examining the use of timeline compression, the section provides readers with insights into how cinematic storytelling necessitates certain adjustments for pacing and emotional impact without sacrificing the core integrity of the narrative.

Composite Characters: Blurring Lines for Narrative Efficiency

In the process of adapting real events, filmmakers often create composite characters— amalgamations of multiple real individuals—to streamline the narrative and reduce the complexity of the cast. This section explores how "Glory Road" employs composite characters, examining the rationale behind these creative choices and their impact on the storytelling dynamics.

The section identifies specific composite characters in the film, delving into how their creation allows for a more focused exploration of key themes. It analyzes the narrative efficiency gained through the use of composite characters, emphasizing how these amalgamations serve the overarching goals of the film. The chapter also reflects on the collaborative effort between the filmmakers, historical consultants, and former players to ensure that the essence of the individuals being portrayed is preserved, even as their stories are intertwined for cinematic purposes. By examining the use of composite characters, the section provides readers with insights into how filmmakers navigate the challenge of condensing complex narratives for cinematic impact while staying true to the spirit of the real events.

Dramatic Flourishes: Enhancing Emotional Resonance

Beyond compression and composite characters, "Glory Road" introduces dramatic flourishes— narrative embellishments designed to enhance emotional resonance and heighten the cinematic experience. This section explores specific instances where the film takes creative liberties for dramatic effect, examining the impact of these embellishments on the audience's emotional connection to the story.

The section identifies key moments in the film where dramatic flourishes are employed, delving into how these embellishments contribute to the overarching themes of the narrative. It analyzes the emotional impact of these creative choices, emphasizing their role in crafting a compelling and resonant cinematic experience. The chapter also reflects on the collaborative effort between the filmmakers, historical consultants, and those directly involved in the events depicted to strike a balance between dramatic storytelling and historical integrity. By examining the use of dramatic flourishes, the section provides readers with insights into how filmmakers leverage creative liberties to evoke powerful emotions and deepen the audience's engagement with the narrative.

The Balancing Act: Maintaining Truth Amidst Creative Choices

As we reflect on the instances of dramatic license in "Glory Road," this section explores the delicate balancing act undertaken by the filmmakers. It considers the challenges of maintaining historical truth while making creative choices that serve the cinematic narrative, emphasizing the responsibility filmmakers feel to honor the legacy of the individuals and events being portrayed.

The section delves into the ethical considerations that inform the filmmakers' decisions, exploring the motivations behind specific creative choices and the impact of those choices on the broader cultural understanding of the Texas Western story. It analyzes how the collaborative effort between the filmmakers, historical consultants, and those directly involved in the events depicted contributes to the delicate balance between historical accuracy and cinematic storytelling. The chapter also reflects on the enduring legacy of "Glory Road" and how its portrayal of events, despite creative liberties, has become an integral part of the cultural narrative surrounding the integration of college basketball in the 1960s. By examining the balancing act between truth and creative choices, the section provides readers with insights into the ethical considerations and responsibilities that shape the intersection of history and cinema.

Conclusion: A Cinematic Tribute to Pioneers

As we conclude our exploration of "Glory Road" and its use of dramatic license with events and timelines, this section reflects on the enduring impact of the film as a cinematic tribute to the pioneers who challenged racial norms within the realm of college basketball. It considers how "Glory Road" contributes to the broader cultural understanding of this transformative moment, acknowledging the artistic choices made by the filmmakers and their role in crafting a narrative that resonates with audiences.

The section reflects on the lasting legacy of "Glory Road," celebrating its place in film history as a compelling and emotionally resonant depiction of a pivotal moment in sports and society. It considers the film's contributions to the broader landscape of sports movies and its unique position in capturing the cultural and historical significance of Texas Western's triumph. The chapter also reflects on the collaborative effort between the filmmakers, historical consultants, and those directly involved in the events depicted, acknowledging the complexities of navigating the intersection of history and cinema. By examining the enduring impact of "Glory Road," the section provides readers with a final appreciation of the film's role as a cinematic tribute to the pioneers who challenged racial norms within the realm of college basketball in the 1960s.

Chapter 9 - Blue Chips (1994)
Nick Nolte as a College Coach Compromised Morally

In the realm of sports dramas, "Blue Chips" stands out as a film that tackles the gritty underbelly of college basketball. At its center is Nick Nolte's complex portrayal of Coach Pete Bell, a character deeply entangled in moral compromises within the cutthroat world of collegiate athletics. This section explores how "Blue Chips" navigates the ethical dilemmas faced by Coach Bell, examining Nick Nolte's nuanced performance and the film's portrayal of the darker side of college sports.

Setting the Stage: The High Stakes of College Recruiting

Before delving into Nick Nolte's portrayal of Coach Pete Bell, this section provides context for the high-stakes world of college basketball recruiting depicted in "Blue Chips." It explores the competitive landscape, the pressures faced by coaches to secure top talent, and the ethical challenges inherent in recruiting young athletes.

The section delves into the backdrop of the film, examining the importance placed on securing star players to maintain a competitive edge. It analyzes the systemic pressures within the college basketball recruiting process, emphasizing the ethical dilemmas faced by coaches as they navigate the blurred lines between fair play and compromising principles. The chapter also reflects on the collaborative effort between the filmmakers and consultants familiar with college athletics to ensure an authentic portrayal of the recruiting environment. By setting the stage for the ethical challenges in "Blue Chips," the section provides readers with insights into the moral quagmire that forms the backdrop of Coach Bell's journey.

Nick Nolte's Coach Pete Bell: A Morally Compromised Figure

This section delves into the heart of "Blue Chips" by examining Nick Nolte's portrayal of Coach Pete Bell. It explores the nuances of the character, the moral compromises he makes, and the internal conflicts that define his journey throughout the film.

The section considers specific scenes that highlight Coach Bell's moral compromises, analyzing Nolte's performance in conveying the internal struggles faced by the character. It examines the complexities of Bell's relationships with players, boosters, and administrators, emphasizing the toll that ethical compromises take on his sense of integrity. The chapter also reflects on the collaborative effort between Nick Nolte, the filmmakers, and sports consultants to create a character that authentically captures the moral dilemmas faced by college coaches. By dissecting Nick Nolte's portrayal of Coach Pete Bell, the section provides readers with insights into the layers of complexity that define the character as a morally compromised figure.

The Recruitment Dilemma: Navigating Unethical Practices

"Blue Chips" shines a spotlight on the unethical practices prevalent in college basketball recruiting. This section explores specific instances within the film where Coach Bell grapples with the pressure to compromise his principles in order to secure top-tier recruits.

The section identifies key recruitment scenes that highlight the moral tightrope walked by Coach Bell, analyzing the choices he faces and the consequences of those choices on the individuals involved. It delves into the film's portrayal of illegal inducements, under-the-table deals, and the exploitation of players for the benefit of the basketball program. The chapter also reflects on the collaborative effort between the filmmakers, consultants, and those with firsthand knowledge of college recruiting to ensure an authentic representation of the ethical challenges faced by coaches. By examining the recruitment dilemma in "Blue Chips," the section provides readers with insights into the pervasive nature of unethical practices within the college basketball landscape.

The Consequences of Compromise: Impact on Players and Program

This section explores the fallout of Coach Bell's moral compromises on both the players under his guidance and the overall integrity of the basketball program. It delves into the consequences of unethical practices portrayed in "Blue Chips," examining the toll on the players' well-being and the broader implications for the program's reputation.

The section considers specific scenes that depict the unraveling of trust between Coach Bell and his players, analyzing the emotional and psychological impact of compromised ethics on the young athletes. It examines the collateral damage inflicted on the basketball program as the consequences of unethical practices come to light. The chapter also reflects on the collaborative effort between the filmmakers, consultants, and individuals with experience in collegiate athletics to ensure a realistic portrayal of the repercussions of moral compromises. By examining the consequences of compromise in "Blue Chips," the section provides readers with insights into the far-reaching effects of ethical lapses within the competitive world of college basketball.

The Redemption Arc: Coach Bell's Journey to Reclaim Integrity

In the latter part of "Blue Chips," Coach Bell embarks on a journey of redemption, seeking to reclaim his integrity and rectify the moral compromises he made. This section explores the film's portrayal of Coach Bell's redemption arc, examining the narrative choices that shape his path toward moral reckoning.

The section identifies key scenes that depict Coach Bell's realization of the ethical quagmire he's entered, analyzing the character's internal struggle and the steps he takes to rectify the situation. It delves into the film's portrayal of redemption within the context of the larger college basketball landscape, exploring the challenges faced by coaches attempting to break free from unethical practices. The chapter also reflects on the collaborative effort between Nick Nolte, the filmmakers, and consultants to authentically capture the emotional and psychological dimensions of Coach Bell's journey toward redemption. By examining Coach Bell's redemption arc, the section provides readers with insights into the film's exploration of ethical accountability and the potential for redemption within the complex world of college athletics.

Cultural Commentary: "Blue Chips" and the Realities of College Sports

As we reflect on Nick Nolte's portrayal of Coach Pete Bell in "Blue Chips," this section explores the cultural commentary embedded in the film. It considers how "Blue Chips" serves as a mirror reflecting the ethical challenges, societal expectations, and systemic issues within the world of college sports.

The section delves into the film's critique of a system that places immense pressure on coaches to win at any cost, examining the societal expectations that contribute to the moral compromises faced by individuals like Coach Bell. It analyzes the broader commentary on the intersection of sports, education, and commerce, emphasizing the film's contribution to the ongoing dialogue surrounding the ethics of collegiate athletics. The chapter also reflects on the collaborative effort between the filmmakers, consultants, and individuals with firsthand experience in college sports to ensure an authentic portrayal of the cultural realities depicted in "Blue Chips." By examining the cultural commentary within the film, the section provides readers with insights into the broader implications of "Blue Chips" as a critical exploration of the ethical landscape of college sports.

Conclusion: "Blue Chips" and the Unending Struggle for Ethical Balance

As we conclude our exploration of "Blue Chips" and Nick Nolte's portrayal of Coach Pete Bell, this section reflects on the enduring impact of the film as a cinematic exploration of the unending struggle for ethical balance within the world of college basketball. It considers how the film's portrayal of moral compromises, redemption, and cultural commentary contributes to the broader conversation about the intersection of sports, ethics, and societal expectations.

The section reflects on the lasting legacy of "Blue Chips," celebrating its place in film history as a thought-provoking examination of the complexities inherent in college athletics. It considers the film's contributions to the broader landscape of sports movies and its unique position in addressing ethical challenges within the competitive realm of collegiate sports. The chapter also reflects on the collaborative effort between Nick Nolte, the filmmakers, and those with expertise in college sports to create a film that resonates with audiences while prompting reflection on the ethical dilemmas faced by coaches. By examining the enduring impact of "Blue Chips," the section provides readers with a final appreciation of the film's role as a cinematic exploration of the perpetual struggle for ethical balance within the dynamic and high-stakes world of college basketball.

Exposing Recruiting Corruption and Ethical Quandaries

"Blue Chips" delves into the murky waters of college basketball recruiting, peeling back the curtain on the high-stakes world where the quest for top-tier talent often collides with ethical boundaries. This section explores how the film exposes the recruiting corruption and ethical quandaries prevalent in the competitive landscape of collegiate athletics.

The Allure of Blue Chip Recruits: The Pressure to Win at Any Cost

Before dissecting the specifics of recruiting corruption in "Blue Chips," this section establishes the broader context of the allure surrounding blue-chip recruits. It delves into the pressures faced by college coaches to secure top-tier talent, examining the competitive landscape that drives programs to pursue star players at almost any cost.

The section analyzes the emphasis placed on blue-chip recruits within the college basketball ecosystem, exploring how their signing is often seen as a critical factor in a program's success. It delves into the systemic pressures that coaches face to consistently secure highly-ranked players, setting the stage for the ethical dilemmas that become central to the film's narrative. By providing an overview of the pressures within the recruiting landscape, the section offers readers insights into the intense competition that forms the backdrop of "Blue Chips."

Recruiting Corruption Unveiled: The Underbelly of Collegiate Athletics

This section takes a closer look at the film's portrayal of recruiting corruption, exposing the underbelly of collegiate athletics. It examines specific scenes and plot points in "Blue Chips" that lay bare the illegal inducements, under-the-table deals, and unethical practices employed by Coach Pete Bell and his coaching peers.

The section identifies key moments in the film where recruiting corruption is unveiled, delving into the methods used by coaches to secure top recruits. It analyzes the film's portrayal of illegal inducements such as cash payments, gifts, and other perks offered to entice players to join a particular program. The chapter also reflects on the collaborative effort between the filmmakers and individuals familiar with the recruiting landscape to ensure an authentic representation of the corrupt practices prevalent in collegiate athletics. By examining the unveiling of recruiting corruption in "Blue Chips," the section provides readers with insights into the film's critical exploration of the ethical quagmire within the competitive world of college basketball.

Ethical Quandaries Faced by Coaches: Balancing Act or Moral Dilemma?

As "Blue Chips" unfolds, it becomes clear that the coaches, including the central character Coach Pete Bell, find themselves entangled in ethical quandaries. This section explores the moral dilemmas faced by coaches as they attempt to balance the pressures of recruiting with the need to maintain integrity.

The section delves into specific scenes that highlight the internal struggles faced by Coach Bell and his coaching peers, analyzing the choices they make and the justifications offered for their actions. It examines the film's portrayal of the fine line between acceptable recruiting practices and outright corruption, emphasizing the internal conflicts that arise as coaches navigate the blurred boundaries. The chapter also reflects on the collaborative effort between the filmmakers and consultants with experience in collegiate athletics to ensure an authentic portrayal of the ethical challenges faced by coaches. By examining the ethical quandaries in "Blue Chips," the section provides readers with insights into the internal struggles that define the characters and contribute to the film's exploration of the ethical dimensions of recruiting in college basketball.

Player Exploitation: The High Cost of Recruiting Success

This section delves into the consequences of recruiting corruption on the players themselves, exploring how the quest for success places young athletes in vulnerable positions. It analyzes specific scenes in "Blue Chips" that depict the exploitation of players for the benefit of the basketball program and the ethical toll this takes on their well-being.

The section identifies key moments in the film where the exploitation of players is showcased, delving into the emotional and psychological impact on the individuals involved. It examines the film's portrayal of the power dynamics between coaches, players, and boosters, emphasizing the high cost paid by young athletes when integrity is sacrificed for recruiting success. The chapter also reflects on the collaborative effort between the filmmakers, consultants, and individuals with firsthand knowledge of collegiate athletics to ensure a realistic representation of the consequences of player exploitation. By examining the portrayal of player exploitation in "Blue Chips," the section provides readers with insights into the human toll exacted by the corrupt practices within the competitive world of college basketball.

The Systemic Issue: "Blue Chips" as a Critique of Collegiate Athletics

Beyond individual instances of recruiting corruption, "Blue Chips" serves as a broader critique of the systemic issues within collegiate athletics. This section explores how the film addresses the cultural norms, institutional pressures, and societal expectations that contribute to the ethical challenges faced by coaches.

The section delves into the film's critique of a system that places immense pressure on coaches to win at any cost, examining how institutional expectations and financial considerations drive the unethical practices depicted in the narrative. It analyzes "Blue Chips" as a cultural commentary on the intersection of sports, education, and commerce, emphasizing the film's contribution to the ongoing dialogue surrounding the ethics of collegiate athletics. The chapter also reflects on the collaborative effort between the filmmakers, consultants, and individuals with firsthand experience in college sports to ensure an authentic portrayal of the systemic issues within collegiate athletics. By examining "Blue Chips" as a critique of the system, the section provides readers with insights into the film's contribution to the broader conversation about the ethical landscape of college sports.

Conclusion: "Blue Chips" and the Unending Struggle for Ethical Reform

As we conclude our exploration of "Blue Chips" and its expose on recruiting corruption and ethical quandaries, this section reflects on the enduring impact of the film as a cinematic exploration of the unending struggle for ethical reform within the world of college basketball. It considers how the film's portrayal of recruiting corruption contributes to the broader conversation about the intersection of sports, ethics, and societal expectations.

The section reflects on the lasting legacy of "Blue Chips," acknowledging its place in film history as a thought-provoking examination of the ethical complexities within collegiate athletics. It considers the film's contributions to the broader landscape of sports movies and its unique position in addressing the need for ethical reform within the competitive realm of collegiate sports. The chapter also reflects on the collaborative effort between the filmmakers, consultants, and those with expertise in college sports to create a film that resonates with audiences while prompting reflection on the ethical dilemmas faced by coaches. By examining the enduring impact of "Blue Chips," the section provides readers with a final appreciation of the film's role as a cinematic exploration of the perpetual struggle for ethical reform within the dynamic and high-stakes world of college basketball.

Cast of NBA Stars and College Talent

"Blue Chips" not only captivates audiences with its exploration of the ethical dilemmas within college basketball but also boasts a remarkable cast featuring both established NBA stars and rising college basketball talents. This section delves into the ensemble cast of "Blue Chips," examining the dynamic performances of the actors, the authenticity they bring to their roles, and the unique collaboration between Hollywood and the basketball world.

NBA Stars Taking Center Stage: Shaquille O'Neal and Penny Hardaway

A significant draw of "Blue Chips" is the inclusion of two basketball superstars, Shaquille O'Neal and Anfernee "Penny" Hardaway, in prominent roles. This section explores how the film leverages the star power of O'Neal and Hardaway, delving into their performances and the impact of their presence on the overall narrative.

The section examines specific scenes featuring Shaquille O'Neal as Neon Boudeaux, a talented and sought-after prospect. It analyzes O'Neal's transition from the basketball court to the silver screen, highlighting his charisma and natural on-screen presence. The chapter also explores Anfernee Hardaway's portrayal of Butch McRae, a talented and conflicted player facing the pressures of college recruitment. It delves into the nuances of Hardaway's performance, considering how his own experiences as a college basketball standout inform his portrayal of Butch. By dissecting the performances of O'Neal and Hardaway, the section provides readers with insights into the casting choices that contribute to the authenticity and appeal of "Blue Chips."

Casting NBA Stars: A Strategic Move or Creative Brilliance?

This section delves into the strategic decision to cast NBA stars in prominent roles within "Blue Chips." It explores the motivations behind this casting choice, considering whether it was primarily a strategic move to draw basketball fans to theaters or a creative decision to infuse authenticity into the film.

The section analyzes the advantages and challenges of casting NBA stars, considering the potential impact on the film's box office success and critical reception. It delves into the unique dynamic created by integrating professional athletes into the world of acting, examining how the casting of O'Neal and Hardaway contributes to the film's overall narrative. The chapter also reflects on the collaborative effort between the filmmakers, casting directors, and basketball consultants to ensure a seamless integration of NBA stars into the fictional world of "Blue Chips." By examining the casting of NBA stars, the section provides readers with insights into the strategic and creative considerations that shaped the film's ensemble.

College Talents on Display: Introducing Future Basketball Stars

In addition to NBA stars, "Blue Chips" introduces audiences to a cast of talented actors portraying college basketball prospects. This section explores the performances of the actors who take on the roles of fictional college recruits, examining how their portrayals contribute to the authenticity of the film's basketball-centric narrative.

The section identifies key characters within the film's ensemble who represent promising college talents, analyzing the performances that bring these characters to life. It delves into the casting choices for these roles, considering how the actors were selected to authentically portray the experiences of young athletes navigating the pressures of recruitment. The chapter also reflects on the collaborative effort between the filmmakers, casting directors, and individuals with experience in college basketball to ensure a realistic representation of the challenges faced by aspiring athletes. By examining the performances of the college talent in "Blue Chips," the section provides readers with insights into the casting decisions that contribute to the film's portrayal of the intense and competitive world of collegiate athletics.

The Interplay Between Hollywood and Hoops: Collaborative Filmmaking

This section explores the collaborative nature of filmmaking in "Blue Chips," considering the interplay between Hollywood professionals and basketball experts. It delves into how the film benefited from the input of consultants, coaches, and players, ensuring that the basketball scenes and overall atmosphere of the film authentically capture the essence of the sport.

The section examines the behind-the-scenes collaboration that took place between the filmmakers and basketball consultants, emphasizing the attention to detail in capturing the nuances of college basketball. It considers how the involvement of individuals with firsthand experience in the basketball world enhanced the realism of the film's depictions of games, practices, and recruitment dynamics. The chapter also reflects on the unique challenges and advantages of creating a sports-centric film that strives for authenticity, acknowledging the contributions of both Hollywood professionals and basketball experts. By examining the collaborative filmmaking process in "Blue Chips," the section provides readers with insights into the careful balance struck between the demands of storytelling and the commitment to capturing the reality of the basketball world.

Impact on Basketball Culture: Hollywood's Influence on the Game

As "Blue Chips" features a cast that includes both NBA stars and emerging talents, this section explores the impact of the film on basketball culture. It considers how Hollywood's portrayal of the sport, combined with the presence of iconic basketball figures, influences the perception of basketball both on and off the court.

The section delves into the film's cultural significance within the basketball community, analyzing how the performances of NBA stars and fictional college recruits contribute to the broader narrative of the sport. It considers the enduring legacy of "Blue Chips" as a film that resonates with basketball enthusiasts, examining its place in the pantheon of sports movies that leave a lasting impact on the culture of the game. The chapter also reflects on the collaborative effort between the filmmakers, consultants, and basketball influencers to create a film that captures the spirit of basketball and leaves an indelible mark on the sport's cultural landscape. By examining the impact of "Blue Chips" on basketball culture, the section provides readers with insights into the lasting influence of the film within the realm of sports entertainment.

Conclusion: "Blue Chips" as a Basketball Cinematic Experience

As we conclude our exploration of the ensemble cast of "Blue Chips," this section reflects on the film's legacy as a basketball cinematic experience. It considers how the casting choices, featuring NBA stars and emerging talents, contribute to the film's authenticity, cultural impact, and enduring appeal within the basketball community.

The section reflects on the lasting legacy of "Blue Chips," celebrating its place in film history as a unique intersection of Hollywood entertainment and the dynamic world of basketball. It considers the film's contributions to the broader landscape of sports movies and its position as a cinematic experience that captures the essence of the sport. The chapter also reflects on the collaborative effort between the filmmakers, casting directors, and basketball experts to create a film that resonates with audiences while authentically portraying the basketball culture. By examining the ensemble cast of "Blue Chips," the section provides readers with a final appreciation of the film's role as a basketball cinematic experience that continues to be cherished by fans and enthusiasts alike.

More Cynical Take on NCAA Machinations

"Blue Chips" takes the audience on a journey into the heart of college basketball, unraveling a narrative that offers a more cynical perspective on the machinations of the NCAA (National Collegiate Athletic Association). This section explores how the film critiques the ethical dilemmas, institutional pressures, and exploitation within the realm of collegiate athletics, presenting a narrative that challenges the traditional portrayal of the NCAA.

The Idealized Image of College Athletics: A Paradigm Under Scrutiny

To contextualize the film's more cynical take on NCAA machinations, this section begins by examining the traditional, idealized image of college athletics. It explores the historical narrative surrounding the NCAA as an institution dedicated to amateurism, education, and the holistic development of student-athletes. The section delves into the romanticized perception of college sports and the associated ideals that have shaped the public's perception of the NCAA.

As "Blue Chips" challenges this idealized image, the section analyzes key scenes and plot points that dismantle the notion of college sports as a pure and amateur endeavor. It delves into the film's portrayal of the pressures faced by coaches, the exploitation of athletes, and the blurred lines between education and sports entertainment. By deconstructing the idealized image of college athletics, the section sets the stage for a deeper exploration of the film's more cynical take on NCAA machinations.

Coaches Caught in the Crossfire: The Pressure to Win at Any Cost

"Blue Chips" portrays the immense pressure faced by college coaches to deliver success on the basketball court. This section explores how the film presents a cynical view of NCAA machinations by depicting coaches as central figures caught in the crossfire of institutional expectations, fan demands, and the quest for victory.

The section analyzes specific scenes that showcase the ethical dilemmas faced by coaches, delving into the choices they make and the compromises they must consider to secure top-tier talent. It examines the film's portrayal of the win-at-all-costs mentality that permeates the collegiate sports landscape, emphasizing the toll it takes on the integrity of coaches and the well-being of athletes. The chapter also reflects on the collaborative effort between the filmmakers, consultants, and individuals with experience in college athletics to ensure an authentic representation of the pressures faced by coaches. By examining the pressures on coaches, the section provides readers with insights into the film's cynical take on the role of coaches in NCAA machinations.

Exploitation of Student-Athletes: The Harsh Reality Behind the Glamour

"Blue Chips" confronts the exploitation of student-athletes within the NCAA system, offering a more cynical perspective on the glamorous facade often associated with collegiate sports. This section explores how the film exposes the harsh reality behind the scenes, where athletes become commodities in a high-stakes game.

The section identifies key moments in the film that highlight the exploitation of student-athletes, delving into scenes that depict the offering of illegal inducements and the compromise of ethical standards. It analyzes the film's portrayal of the transactional nature of college recruitment, emphasizing the commodification of athletes in the pursuit of victory. The chapter also reflects on the collaborative effort between the filmmakers, consultants, and individuals with firsthand knowledge of college sports to ensure a realistic representation of the challenges faced by student-athletes. By examining the exploitation of athletes, the section provides readers with insights into the film's more cynical take on the treatment of student-athletes within NCAA machinations.

NCAA as a Business: The Profit Motive Behind College Sports

"Blue Chips" digs deeper into the economic underpinnings of college sports, presenting a narrative that views the NCAA as a business entity driven by profit motives. This section explores how the film challenges the perception of collegiate athletics as a purely amateur endeavor, shedding light on the financial interests that shape the NCAA landscape.

The section analyzes specific scenes in the film that depict the financial pressures faced by college programs, delving into the portrayal of boosters, sponsors, and the economic forces that influence decision-making. It examines the film's critique of the NCAA as an organization that prioritizes revenue generation over the well-being of student-athletes. The chapter also reflects on the collaborative effort between the filmmakers, consultants, and individuals with expertise in sports economics to ensure an authentic representation of the financial dynamics within college sports. By examining the profit motive behind college sports, the section provides readers with insights into the film's more cynical take on the economic machinations of the NCAA.

Academic Compromises: When Sports Trump Education

This section explores how "Blue Chips" navigates the theme of academic compromises within NCAA machinations. It delves into the film's portrayal of the delicate balance between academic pursuits and athletic success, presenting a more cynical view of how educational standards may be compromised in the pursuit of sports glory.

The section analyzes specific scenes that depict academic compromises, examining the challenges faced by student-athletes in balancing their studies with the demands of their sport. It explores the film's critique of a system where athletes may be nudged toward academic shortcuts to maintain eligibility. The chapter also reflects on the collaborative effort between the filmmakers, consultants, and individuals with experience in college academics to ensure a realistic representation of the academic challenges faced by student-athletes. By examining academic compromises, the section provides readers with insights into the film's more cynical take on the intersection of education and athletics within NCAA machinations.

Media Scrutiny and Scandals: The Dark Side of NCAA Exposed

"Blue Chips" sheds light on the media scrutiny and scandals that often accompany NCAA machinations, revealing a darker side to the glamorous world of college sports. This section explores how the film presents a more cynical view of the media's role in exposing the ethical dilemmas and controversies within collegiate athletics.

The section analyzes specific scenes that depict media scrutiny, examining the consequences of scandals and the impact on coaches, athletes, and the reputation of college programs. It explores the film's portrayal of the delicate relationship between the NCAA, the media, and public perception. The chapter also reflects on the collaborative effort between the filmmakers, consultants, and individuals with experience in sports journalism to ensure an authentic representation of the media dynamics within college sports. By examining media scrutiny and scandals, the section provides readers with insights into the film's more cynical take on the external forces that shape NCAA machinations.

Conclusion: "Blue Chips" and the Unmasking of NCAA Realities

As we conclude our exploration of "Blue Chips" and its more cynical take on NCAA machinations, this section reflects on the enduring impact of the film as a cinematic unmasking of the realities within the world of college basketball. It considers how the film's portrayal of ethical dilemmas, exploitation, economic interests, academic compromises, and media scrutiny contributes to the broader conversation about the complexities and challenges faced by the NCAA.

The section reflects on the lasting legacy of "Blue Chips," acknowledging its place in film history as a thought-provoking examination of the ethical complexities within collegiate athletics. It considers the film's contributions to the broader landscape of sports movies and its unique position in addressing the need for ethical reform within the competitive realm of college basketball. The chapter also reflects on the collaborative effort between the filmmakers, consultants, and those with expertise in college sports to create a film that resonates with audiences while prompting reflection on the ethical dilemmas faced by coaches and athletes. By examining the more cynical take on NCAA machinations in "Blue Chips," the section provides readers with a final appreciation of the film's role as a cinematic exploration of the perpetual struggle for ethical reform within the dynamic and high-stakes world of college basketball.

Chapter 10 - Hoop Dreams (1994)
Steve James' Landmark Documentary Following Two Preps

"Hoop Dreams," a groundbreaking documentary directed by Steve James, transcends the traditional boundaries of sports filmmaking. In this section, we delve into the meticulous craft and storytelling brilliance of Steve James as he brings to life the raw and compelling narratives of two aspiring young basketball players, Arthur Agee and William Gates.

Setting the Stage: The Documentary Landscape in the '90s

Before delving into the specifics of "Hoop Dreams," this section provides a contextual overview of the documentary landscape in the 1990s. It explores the factors that shaped the era's documentary filmmaking, highlighting the increasing popularity of the genre and the evolving techniques employed by filmmakers to tell compelling, real-life stories. This introduction sets the stage for understanding the unique position occupied by "Hoop Dreams" within the documentary landscape of its time.

The Genesis of "Hoop Dreams": Steve James' Vision and Approach

This subsection unravels the inception of "Hoop Dreams" and the vision that director Steve James brought to the project. It explores James' background, his previous works, and how his unique perspective influenced the storytelling approach of the documentary. By delving into James' filmmaking philosophy and choices, the section sets the foundation for understanding the distinctive qualities that make "Hoop Dreams" a landmark documentary.

Two Preps, One Dream: Arthur Agee and William Gates

At the heart of "Hoop Dreams" are the intertwined journeys of Arthur Agee and William Gates, two young African American basketball players from inner-city Chicago. This part of the section delves into the personal stories of Agee and Gates, exploring their backgrounds, aspirations, and the challenges they face as they navigate the competitive landscape of high school basketball. It also examines how Steve James builds a deep and empathetic connection between the audience and the two protagonists, making their dreams and struggles universally resonant.

The Cinéma Vérité Style: Capturing Reality Unfolding

"Hoop Dreams" adopts a cinéma vérité style, immersing viewers in the unscripted and unpredictable realities of the lives of Agee and Gates. This subsection analyzes the use of cinéma vérité in the documentary, exploring how it captures the authenticity of the subjects' experiences. It also delves into the challenges and triumphs of adopting this observational approach, providing a lens into the daily lives, triumphs, and setbacks of the two aspiring athletes.

Narrative Arcs and Structural Brilliance

Steve James weaves a narrative tapestry that goes beyond the basketball court, encompassing broader themes of socio-economic challenges, race, and the pursuit of the American Dream. This part of the section dissects the narrative arcs of Agee and Gates, examining how James structures the documentary to create a compelling and emotionally resonant story. It explores the thematic depth that emerges as the documentary progresses, providing insights into the layered storytelling that distinguishes "Hoop Dreams."

Challenges and Triumphs: The Realities of Pursuing Dreams

The documentary captures the harsh realities and challenges faced by Agee and Gates as they navigate the complexities of high school, basketball, and life in inner-city Chicago. This subsection analyzes key moments in the documentary that highlight the triumphs and setbacks experienced by the two protagonists. It explores the emotional impact of these moments and their significance in portraying the human side of the pursuit of basketball dreams.

Critically Lauded: Reception and Impact of "Hoop Dreams"

"Hoop Dreams" received widespread critical acclaim and became a cultural phenomenon. This part of the section examines the reception of the documentary, exploring how it was embraced by audiences, critics, and the film industry. It delves into the awards and accolades garnered by "Hoop Dreams" and its lasting impact on documentary filmmaking, sports storytelling, and the broader cultural conversation.

The Legacy of "Hoop Dreams": Influencing Documentaries and Beyond

"Hoop Dreams" didn't just end with its release; it left an indelible mark on the documentary genre and beyond. This subsection explores the legacy of "Hoop Dreams," examining its influence on subsequent documentaries, filmmakers, and the broader cultural discourse. It considers how the documentary continues to be relevant and resonant, contributing to ongoing conversations about race, socio-economic disparities, and the pursuit of dreams.

Conclusion: "Hoop Dreams" and the Power of Human Stories

As we conclude our exploration of "Hoop Dreams," this section reflects on the enduring power of human stories and the transformative potential of documentary filmmaking. It considers how Steve James, through his visionary approach, elevated a basketball documentary into a timeless exploration of the human spirit. The chapter also reflects on the collaborative effort between James, the subjects, and the filmmaking team to create a documentary that transcends the genre, leaving a lasting impact on both sports and storytelling. By examining "Hoop Dreams," the section provides readers with a final appreciation of the documentary's significance as a testament to the resilience, dreams, and complexities of the human experience.

Epic Runtime Allows Thorough Look at Challenges and Inequity

"Hoop Dreams," a cinematic masterpiece directed by Steve James, unfolds as a marathon exploration of the challenges and inequities inherent in the pursuit of basketball dreams by inner-city youth. This section delves into the epic runtime of the documentary, analyzing how its extended duration allows for an unparalleled depth of examination into the lives of Arthur Agee and William Gates.

The Pioneering Decision: Embracing Epic Length for Documentary Storytelling

Before delving into the impact of the epic runtime, this part of the section examines the groundbreaking decision by Steve James to embrace an extended duration for "Hoop Dreams." It explores the director's motivations, challenges, and the unique narrative opportunities afforded by a documentary that spans over three hours. This introduction sets the stage for understanding the unconventional yet transformative approach taken by James in telling the stories of Agee and Gates.

Immersion into Realities: A Day-in-the-Life Approach

The extended runtime of "Hoop Dreams" allows for an immersive day-in-the-life approach, providing an unfiltered and intimate look at the struggles, triumphs, and ordinary moments in the lives of Agee and Gates. This subsection explores how the documentary's length enables viewers to step into the shoes of the protagonists, experiencing the challenges of their daily existence and the gradual evolution of their dreams. It delves into specific scenes and sequences that benefit from the prolonged duration, creating a visceral connection between the audience and the subjects.

Navigating Complex Narratives: Layered Storytelling Unfolds

The documentary's extended duration facilitates layered storytelling, allowing for the exploration of multiple narratives and themes. This part of the section analyzes how Steve James navigates the complex narratives of Agee and Gates, delving into their family dynamics, socio-economic challenges, and the broader societal issues that shape their journeys. It examines specific narrative arcs that benefit from the extended runtime, providing a nuanced and comprehensive understanding of the protagonists and their environments.

A Chronicle of Inequity: Socio-Economic Realities Laid Bare

The epic runtime becomes a narrative canvas for laying bare the socio-economic inequities that permeate the lives of Agee and Gates. This subsection explores how the documentary meticulously chronicles the challenges faced by the protagonists, from navigating underfunded schools to dealing with the harsh realities of inner-city life. It analyzes specific scenes and moments that capture the systemic inequities, allowing the documentary to transcend the basketball narrative and become a poignant commentary on societal disparities.

Longitudinal Filmmaking: Evolving Characters and Themes

"Hoop Dreams" distinguishes itself through the use of longitudinal filmmaking, capturing the evolution of characters and themes over an extended period. This part of the section delves into how the documentary spans several years, showcasing the growth, setbacks, and transformations experienced by Agee and Gates. It examines specific moments that benefit from the longitudinal approach, offering viewers a unique perspective on the passage of time and the dynamic nature of the protagonists' journeys.

Emotional Resonance: Building Deep Connections with Subjects

The extended runtime contributes to the emotional resonance of "Hoop Dreams," allowing viewers to forge deep connections with Agee and Gates. This subsection explores how the documentary's length creates space for moments of vulnerability, joy, heartbreak, and resilience. It analyzes scenes that evoke powerful emotional responses, showcasing the impact of the extended duration on the audience's engagement with the subjects.

The Documentary as Cultural Artifact: Comprehensive Examination

The extended runtime of "Hoop Dreams" transforms the documentary into a cultural artifact, offering a comprehensive examination of the socio-economic, racial, and educational challenges faced by inner-city youth. This part of the section explores how the documentary goes beyond the basketball court, becoming a window into the broader issues that shape the protagonists' lives. It considers the impact of the extended duration on the documentary's role as a cultural document, influencing discussions about race, class, and the American Dream.

Critical Acclaim and Enduring Influence: The Legacy of Lengthy Exploration

"Hoop Dreams" received critical acclaim for its lengthy exploration, and this subsection examines the reception and lasting influence of the documentary. It explores how the extended runtime contributed to the film's recognition, awards, and its enduring status as a touchstone in documentary filmmaking. It reflects on the collaborative effort between the filmmakers, the subjects, and the audience, acknowledging the shared journey facilitated by the documentary's epic duration.

Conclusion: The Enduring Impact of Prolonged Reflection

As we conclude our exploration of "Hoop Dreams" and its epic runtime, this section reflects on the enduring impact of prolonged reflection. It considers how the extended duration of the documentary allows for a thorough examination of challenges, inequities, and the resilience of the human spirit. The chapter also reflects on the collaborative effort between Steve James, the subjects, and the audience, acknowledging the shared commitment to a cinematic journey that goes beyond the constraints of time. By examining the epic runtime of "Hoop Dreams," the section provides readers with a final appreciation of the documentary's lasting significance as a testament to the power of in-depth exploration and storytelling.

Critically Lauded as a Work of Social Commentary

"Hoop Dreams," directed by Steve James, is not merely a basketball documentary; it stands as a monumental work of social commentary. In this section, we dissect the critical acclaim and recognition bestowed upon the documentary for its incisive exploration of broader societal issues, making it a cultural touchstone that transcends the realm of sports filmmaking.

Contextualizing Social Commentary in Sports Documentaries

Before delving into the social commentary within "Hoop Dreams," this part of the section sets the stage by contextualizing the role of social commentary in sports documentaries. It explores how filmmakers use the backdrop of sports to delve into deeper societal issues, providing an overview of the genre's evolution and the increasing recognition of documentaries as powerful tools for social critique.

Hoop Dreams Beyond the Court: Unearthing Socio-Economic Realities

"Hoop Dreams" unfolds as a profound social commentary by lifting the veil on the socio-economic realities faced by its protagonists, Arthur Agee and William Gates. This subsection delves into how the documentary serves as a window into the challenges of inner-city life, addressing systemic issues such as poverty, inadequate education, and the scarcity of opportunities. It analyzes specific scenes and sequences that underscore the documentary's commitment to shedding light on the broader social context that shapes the dreams and struggles of its central characters.

Race and the American Dream: A Nuanced Exploration

One of the standout features of "Hoop Dreams" is its nuanced exploration of race and the American Dream. This part of the section dissects how the documentary navigates the complex intersection of race, class, and opportunity, providing a platform for viewers to engage with the systemic challenges faced by African American youth pursuing their dreams. It examines specific instances where the documentary delves into racial dynamics, fostering a deeper understanding of the societal context in which Agee and Gates strive for success.

Educational Disparities: Inner-city Schools Under the Lens

An integral component of the social commentary within "Hoop Dreams" is the scrutiny of educational disparities. This subsection explores how the documentary shines a spotlight on the challenges within the education system, particularly in underfunded inner-city schools. It analyzes scenes that highlight the struggles faced by Agee and Gates in pursuing their education alongside their basketball aspirations, contributing to a broader discourse on the systemic barriers to academic achievement.

Family Dynamics: The Impact of Socio-Economic Pressures

"Hoop Dreams" goes beyond the basketball court to examine the intricate dynamics of the protagonists' families, revealing the impact of socio-economic pressures on familial relationships. This part of the section delves into how the documentary portrays the strains on familial bonds, exploring how economic hardships and societal expectations intersect with personal aspirations. It examines key moments that illuminate the complex interplay between individual dreams and the collective well-being of the family unit.

The Invisible Hoops: Systemic Challenges for Inner-city Youth

The documentary transcends its immediate focus on basketball, addressing the invisible hoops that inner-city youth must navigate. This subsection explores how "Hoop Dreams" unveils the systemic challenges—from institutional racism to economic disparities—that create metaphorical hoops for individuals like Agee and Gates. It analyzes specific instances that underscore the metaphorical nature of these invisible barriers, providing viewers with a thought-provoking commentary on the broader societal obstacles faced by marginalized communities.

Critics' Acclaim: Recognizing the Power of Commentary

"Hoop Dreams" received widespread acclaim from critics, and this part of the section examines the reviews and commentary that recognized the documentary's power as a social commentary. It explores how critics lauded the film for its unflinching portrayal of societal issues, acknowledging the impact of its narrative depth and the thought-provoking questions it raises. The subsection considers specific critical responses that highlight the documentary's significance in pushing the boundaries of sports filmmaking.

Awards and Nominations: Acknowledging Social Impact

The accolades garnered by "Hoop Dreams" further underscore its status as a work of social commentary. This subsection delves into the awards and nominations received by the documentary, exploring how the recognition from prestigious institutions and festivals acknowledged its impact as a cultural touchstone. It reflects on the collective acknowledgment of the documentary's ability to spark important conversations about race, education, and the American Dream.

Enduring Impact: Social Commentary Beyond the '90s

"Hoop Dreams" continues to be relevant as a work of social commentary beyond its initial release. This part of the section examines how the documentary's impact has endured, influencing subsequent filmmakers, educators, and activists. It considers the ongoing relevance of its themes and the documentary's place in discussions about systemic issues in contemporary society.

Conclusion: The Lasting Reverberations of "Hoop Dreams"

As we conclude our exploration of "Hoop Dreams" as a critically lauded work of social commentary, this section reflects on the lasting reverberations of the documentary. It considers how the film's commentary on race, socio-economic disparities, and the pursuit of dreams continues to resonate with audiences. By examining "Hoop Dreams" through the lens of social commentary, the section provides readers with a final appreciation of the documentary's enduring significance as a cinematic force that transcends the boundaries of sports and speaks to the heart of societal challenges.

Influential Depiction of NBA Aspirations and Reality

"Hoop Dreams" doesn't merely document the journey of two aspiring basketball players; it offers a profound exploration of NBA aspirations and the stark reality that often accompanies the pursuit of such dreams. This section dissects the documentary's influential depiction of the NBA as a symbol of aspiration, examining the challenges, sacrifices, and triumphs faced by Arthur Agee and William Gates.

The NBA Dream as a Driving Force: Aspiration and Inspiration

Before delving into the challenges, this part of the section explores how "Hoop Dreams" presents the NBA dream as a powerful driving force for young athletes like Agee and Gates. It delves into the allure of NBA stardom, examining the cultural and societal factors that make the league a symbol of aspiration and inspiration for countless aspiring players. By capturing the initial allure of the NBA dream, the documentary sets the stage for a nuanced exploration of the realities that follow.

The Illusion of Overnight Success: Navigating the High School Spotlight

"Hoop Dreams" sheds light on the illusion of overnight success often associated with NBA aspirations, especially in the context of high school basketball. This subsection analyzes how the documentary navigates the challenges of the high school spotlight, exploring the pressures, expectations, and scrutiny faced by Agee and Gates as they become local basketball stars. It dissects specific scenes that highlight the complexities of being thrust into the limelight at a young age, offering a glimpse into the transformative power of the NBA dream and the burdens it can carry.

The NCAA as a Stepping Stone: Hurdles on the Path to the NBA

For many aspiring basketball players, the NCAA represents a crucial stepping stone towards realizing NBA dreams. This part of the section examines how "Hoop Dreams" portrays the challenges and hurdles associated with the college basketball journey. It analyzes the documentary's depiction of the NCAA as both a gateway to professional basketball and a landscape fraught with ethical dilemmas, exploitative practices, and intense competition. By delving into the college basketball experience, the documentary provides a comprehensive view of the multifaceted path to the NBA.

Inequities in College Athletics: The Struggle for Recognition and Fair Compensation

"Hoop Dreams" doesn't shy away from addressing the inequities within college athletics, offering a critical lens on the struggle for recognition and fair compensation. This subsection explores how the documentary captures the challenges faced by Agee and Gates as they navigate the complex world of college basketball. It analyzes specific scenes that underscore the disparity between the lucrative business of college sports and the limited agency and compensation afforded to the athletes. By tackling issues of exploitation and inequity, the documentary contributes to a broader discourse on the relationship between college athletes and the institutions they represent.

Injuries and Setbacks: The Fragility of NBA Aspirations

The path to the NBA is fraught with physical demands, and "Hoop Dreams" doesn't shy away from portraying the fragility of NBA aspirations in the face of injuries and setbacks. This part of the section examines how the documentary captures the impact of injuries on Agee and Gates, revealing the harsh reality that injuries can shatter dreams and alter the trajectory of promising careers. It analyzes specific moments that showcase the vulnerability of aspiring athletes and the emotional toll of facing unexpected obstacles on the journey to the NBA.

Family Sacrifices: The Cost of Chasing NBA Dreams

NBA aspirations come at a cost, not just for the players but for their families as well. This subsection explores how "Hoop Dreams" delves into the sacrifices made by the families of Agee and Gates as they support their sons' pursuit of NBA dreams. It analyzes specific scenes that highlight the emotional and financial burdens carried by the families, shedding light on the interconnectedness of personal aspirations and familial support. By portraying the impact on family dynamics, the documentary adds layers of complexity to the narrative of NBA aspirations.

The NBA Draft: Anticipation, Hope, and Harsh Realities

For aspiring basketball players, the NBA Draft represents the culmination of years of hard work and dedication. This part of the section dissects how "Hoop Dreams" captures the anticipation, hope, and harsh realities associated with the NBA Draft. It examines the documentary's portrayal of the draft as a pivotal moment that can either validate the dreams of aspiring players or usher in a sobering realization of the challenges that lie ahead. By exploring the emotional rollercoaster of the draft process, the documentary provides viewers with a poignant look at the intersection of aspiration and reality.

Life After the Dream: Navigating Disappointment and Resilience

Not every player realizes their NBA dream, and "Hoop Dreams" acknowledges the harsh reality of life after the dream. This subsection explores how the documentary navigates the disappointment, resilience, and determination of Agee and Gates as they confront the challenges of transitioning from the height of their basketball aspirations. It analyzes specific scenes that capture the essence of resilience, showcasing how the documentary goes beyond the court to explore the enduring spirit of those who navigate life after NBA dreams.

Legacy and Inspiration: Beyond the Personal Journey

The influence of "Hoop Dreams" extends beyond the personal journeys of Agee and Gates; it serves as a source of inspiration and reflection for countless individuals. This part of the section examines how the documentary's depiction of NBA aspirations and reality contributes to a broader legacy of inspiration. It reflects on the enduring impact of the film in shaping conversations about the pursuit of dreams, the complexities of the sports industry, and the resilience required to navigate the challenges of life beyond the court.

Conclusion: "Hoop Dreams" and the Ever-Persistent NBA Aspiration

As we conclude our exploration of "Hoop Dreams" and its influential depiction of NBA aspirations and reality, this section reflects on the ever-persistent nature of the NBA dream. It considers how the documentary's nuanced portrayal of the challenges, sacrifices, and triumphs associated with NBA aspirations contributes to a richer understanding of the enduring allure of professional basketball. By examining "Hoop Dreams" through the lens of NBA aspirations and reality, the section provides readers with a final appreciation of the documentary's timeless significance as a narrative that resonates with the universal pursuit of dreams and the complex realities that accompany them.

Chapter 11 - Hardwood Themes: Comparing Cinematic Depictions

Varied Representations of Race, Gender, and Culture

In the realm of basketball cinema, the representations of race, gender, and culture are integral components that shape the narratives and resonate with audiences. This section explores how the selected films in this book—each a distinct piece in the mosaic of basketball storytelling—contribute to a rich tapestry of perspectives on race, gender, and culture. Through a comparative lens, we examine the nuanced portrayals, challenges, and progress reflected in these cinematic depictions.

Race on the Hardwood: Diverse Narratives and Cultural Perspectives

Basketball, as a sport deeply embedded in American culture, serves as a lens through which filmmakers explore diverse narratives of race. This subsection delves into how each film in this collection uniquely approaches the representation of race. From the inner-city struggles depicted in "Hoop Dreams" to the racial tensions of college basketball in "Glory Road," we dissect the films' storytelling choices, character dynamics, and societal reflections. By comparing these narratives, we gain insights into the evolving cinematic landscape and its ability to confront and challenge prevailing racial narratives.

Breaking Gender Barriers: Women in Basketball Cinema

While basketball has often been associated with male athletes, a notable shift has occurred in recent decades with an increased focus on women's contributions to the sport. This part of the section explores how the selected films depict women in the basketball world. From the powerful portrayal of Monica and Quincy's journey in "Love & Basketball" to Whoopi Goldberg's comedic turn in "Eddie," we analyze how these films contribute to breaking gender barriers. By comparing the representation of female characters, athletes, and coaches, we gain a deeper understanding of the evolving role of women in basketball cinema.

Cultural Crossroads: Exploring Diversity and Inclusion

Basketball, as a global phenomenon, transcends cultural boundaries, and the films in this collection reflect this cultural diversity. This subsection delves into how the selected films navigate cultural crossroads, exploring the intersectionality of race, ethnicity, and nationality. From the multicultural dynamics in "White Men Can't Jump" to the examination of racial tensions in "He Got Game," we analyze how these films contribute to a broader conversation about diversity and inclusion. By comparing the cultural nuances depicted in each film, we gain insights into how basketball cinema serves as a platform for exploring the complexities of identity and belonging.

Challenging Stereotypes: Racial and Gender Dynamics in Film Duos

One of the unique features of basketball cinema is the exploration of dynamic duos, whether in friendships, partnerships, or mentorships. This part of the section examines how these cinematic duos contribute to challenging stereotypes related to race and gender. From the unexpected bond in "White Men Can't Jump" to the convict-father and phenom-son dynamic in "He Got Game," we analyze the power dynamics, chemistry, and challenges faced by these duos. By comparing these relationships, we uncover how basketball cinema navigates complex societal expectations and stereotypes.

Intersectionality in Focus: Layered Identities on the Court

Intersectionality—the interconnected nature of social categorizations such as race, gender, and class—is a key theme explored in these films. This subsection delves into how the films navigate the layered identities of their characters, particularly those at the intersection of multiple social categories. From the nuanced exploration of love and aspiration in "Love & Basketball" to the examination of racial and economic complexities in "Blue Chips," we analyze how these films tackle intersectionality. By comparing the layered identities depicted in each film, we gain insights into the narrative richness and societal reflections embedded in basketball cinema.

Evolution of Representation: From Stereotypes to Authenticity

Over the years, basketball cinema has undergone an evolution in its representation of race, gender, and culture. This part of the section explores this evolution, tracing the shift from early stereotypes to more authentic and nuanced portrayals. From the groundbreaking representation in "Hoop Dreams" to the reimagining of coach dynamics in "Coach Carter," we analyze how these films contribute to reshaping cinematic narratives. By comparing the evolution of representation, we gain a deeper understanding of the transformative power of basketball cinema in challenging and reshaping societal norms.

Cinematic Impact: Beyond the Hardwood and Into Society

The impact of cinematic representations extends beyond the confines of the movie screen, influencing societal perceptions and conversations. This subsection explores how the selected films contribute to broader discussions about race, gender, and culture. From the enduring influence of "Hoop Dreams" as a social commentary to the redefining of sports movie tropes in "Coach Carter," we analyze how these films resonate with audiences and shape cultural narratives. By comparing the cinematic impact of each film, we gain insights into the enduring influence of basketball cinema on societal conversations.

Conclusion: The Ever-Evolving Tapestry of Basketball Cinema

As we conclude our exploration of varied representations of race, gender, and culture in basketball cinema, this section reflects on the ever-evolving tapestry of storytelling. It considers how each film contributes to a dynamic and multifaceted narrative that transcends the boundaries of the hardwood. By comparing the nuanced depictions of race, gender, and culture, the section provides readers with a final appreciation of basketball cinema as a mirror reflecting the complexities, challenges, and triumphs of the human experience on and off the court.

Characters United by Hoop Dreams and Obstacles

In the realm of basketball cinema, a common thread weaves through disparate narratives—the unifying power of hoop dreams. This section explores how the selected films bring characters together through shared aspirations, facing a myriad of obstacles on their journeys. By delving into the diverse portrayals of characters united by their passion for basketball, we uncover the nuanced ways in which these films depict the transformative and communal nature of the sport.

The Shared Language of the Court: Basketball as a Unifying Force

At the heart of these films lies a shared language—the game of basketball. This subsection explores how characters from different backgrounds, experiences, and walks of life are brought together by their shared love for the sport. From the inner-city courts of "Hoop Dreams" to the pickup games in "White Men Can't Jump," we analyze how basketball becomes a unifying force that transcends societal divides. By comparing the diverse settings and character dynamics, we gain insights into the transformative power of the court in fostering connections and overcoming obstacles.

Friendship Forged in the Crucible: Bonds Beyond the Hardwood

Many basketball films explore friendships forged in the crucible of competition and shared dreams. This part of the section delves into how characters form deep and enduring connections beyond the hardwood. From the complex bond between Monica and Quincy in "Love & Basketball" to the unlikely partnership of Sidney and Billy in "White Men Can't

Jump," we analyze how these friendships shape the characters' journeys. By comparing the dynamics of these relationships, we uncover the thematic richness of friendship as a central element in basketball cinema.

Mentorship and Guidance: Navigating Obstacles with a Wise Figure

The journey toward realizing hoop dreams is often fraught with obstacles, and characters frequently find guidance from mentors who offer wisdom and support. This subsection explores how mentorship is depicted in the selected films, examining the relationships between seasoned players and those aspiring to follow in their footsteps. From the convict-father and phenom-son dynamic in "He Got Game" to the coaching influence in "Coach Carter," we analyze the transformative impact of mentorship. By comparing these mentor-mentee dynamics, we gain insights into the ways in which guidance shapes character development and resilience.

Familial Bonds: Basketball as a Family Affair

For some characters, basketball is not just a personal pursuit—it becomes a family affair. This part of the section delves into how familial bonds are woven into the narratives, exploring the dynamics of characters whose hoop dreams intertwine with family aspirations. From the underdog family in "Hoosiers" to the familial struggles in "Hoop Dreams," we analyze how the familial context adds layers of complexity to the characters' journeys. By comparing these portrayals, we gain insights into the intersecting dynamics of family, basketball, and the pursuit of dreams.

Rivalries and Team Dynamics: The Agony and Ecstasy of Competition

The competitive nature of basketball brings forth both agonizing rivalries and euphoric team dynamics. This subsection explores how characters navigate the highs and lows of competition, from intense rivalries in "Hoosiers" to the team-building process in "Glory Road." Analyzing the ways in which characters unite or clash on the court, we uncover the emotional depth and complexity of the competitive spirit. By comparing these dynamics, we gain insights into how competition serves as a catalyst for character growth and collective resilience.

Overcoming Adversity: The Triumph of the Human Spirit

Obstacles are inherent in any journey, and characters in these films face adversity that tests the limits of their resilience. This part of the section delves into how characters overcome challenges, examining the triumph of the human spirit in the face of adversity. From the academic struggles in "Coach Carter" to the racial tensions in "Glory Road," we analyze how characters rise above obstacles. By comparing these narratives, we gain insights into the ways in which basketball cinema celebrates the indomitable human spirit and its ability to persevere.

Individual vs. Collective Dreams: Balancing Personal Aspirations and Team Goals

The tension between individual aspirations and collective team goals is a recurring theme in basketball cinema. This subsection explores how characters navigate the delicate balance between personal dreams and the dynamics of teamwork. From the individual pursuits in "He Got Game" to the team-building in "Glory Road," we analyze how characters grapple with the tension between self-interest and collective success. By comparing these narratives, we gain insights into the nuanced ways in which basketball cinema explores the complexities of balancing individuality within a team context.

Legacy and Impact: Characters Beyond the Screen

The impact of characters extends beyond the confines of the movie screen, shaping cultural conversations and leaving a lasting legacy. This part of the section explores how the characters in these films contribute to a broader cultural narrative. From the enduring legacy of "Hoop Dreams" to the cultural impact of characters like Billy Hoyle in "White Men Can't Jump," we analyze how these characters resonate with audiences and influence societal perceptions. By comparing the cultural impact of each character, we gain insights into the enduring power of basketball cinema in shaping collective imaginations.

Conclusion: Characters United in the Pantheon of Basketball Cinema

As we conclude our exploration of characters united by hoop dreams and obstacles, this section reflects on the pantheon of basketball cinema and the diverse characters that inhabit it. It considers how these characters, with their shared aspirations and individual challenges, contribute to a collective narrative that transcends the boundaries of the screen. By comparing the character dynamics, relationships, and transformative journeys, the section provides readers with a final appreciation of basketball cinema as a storyteller that weaves together the rich tapestry of the human experience.

Examining Narrative Tropes Across Genres

In the cinematic world of basketball, various genres converge to tell stories that transcend the boundaries of sports. This section delves into the narrative tropes employed across genres within basketball cinema. From documentaries to comedies, dramas to biopics, we examine the ways in which filmmakers utilize distinct storytelling techniques to capture the essence of the sport and its impact on the human experience.

Documentary Realism: The Power of Unscripted Narratives

Documentaries, with their commitment to unscripted storytelling, offer an authentic lens into the world of basketball. This subsection explores how documentaries like "Hoop Dreams" and "Hoop Dreams 2" embrace realism to capture the challenges, triumphs, and aspirations of individuals within the basketball community. We analyze the unique power of unscripted narratives in conveying a genuine and unfiltered representation of the sport, providing audiences with an intimate look at the lives and dreams of those involved.

Sports Drama: The Heroic Journey on the Hardwood

The sports drama genre has long been a staple in basketball cinema, offering narratives that follow the heroic journey of athletes and teams. This part of the section examines how films like "Hoosiers" and "Glory Road" employ the classic elements of the hero's journey to create compelling and emotionally resonant stories. We analyze the ways in which sports dramas use underdog narratives, coaching dynamics, and the quest for victory to evoke a range of emotions and connect with audiences on a visceral level.

Comedic Interplay: Laughter on the Court

Comedy, an unexpected yet vibrant genre within basketball cinema, injects humor into the often intense world of sports. This subsection explores how films like "White Men Can't Jump" and "Eddie" use comedic elements to entertain audiences while navigating the challenges and triumphs of the basketball world. We analyze the comedic interplay, witty dialogues, and character dynamics that infuse levity into the genre, demonstrating the diverse ways in which basketball stories can be told with humor and wit.

Biographical Narratives: Real Lives, Real Impact

Biopics provide a platform to explore the real lives of basketball legends and the impact they've had on the sport and society. This part of the section delves into how films like "He Got Game" and "Coach Carter" use biographical narratives to depict the struggles, successes, and personal journeys of iconic figures. We analyze the ways in which biopics capture the essence of real-life stories, portraying the indomitable spirit of individuals who left an enduring mark on the basketball landscape.

Cultural Commentary: Basketball as a Mirror of Society

Some basketball films transcend the genre to become poignant cultural commentaries. This subsection explores how films like "Blue Chips" and "Love & Basketball" use the sport as a mirror reflecting broader societal issues. We analyze the cultural nuances, social commentaries, and explorations of race, gender, and ethics embedded in these films, showcasing how basketball cinema can serve as a powerful tool for societal reflection and critique.

Coming-of-Age Tales: Basketball and the Journey to Adulthood

Coming-of-age narratives within basketball cinema explore the transformative journey from adolescence to adulthood. This part of the section examines how films like "Love & Basketball" and "He Got Game" use the sport as a backdrop for characters navigating the challenges of growing up. We analyze the ways in which coming-of-age tales within basketball cinema capture the universal themes of identity, love, and self-discovery, providing audiences with relatable and emotionally charged narratives.

Social Justice and Advocacy: Basketball as a Platform for Change

In recent years, basketball cinema has increasingly become a platform for social justice and advocacy narratives. This subsection explores how films like "Hoop Dreams" and "Coach Carter" tackle issues of inequality, education, and systemic challenges within the basketball community. We analyze the ways in which these films amplify social justice messages, using the sport as a catalyst for positive change and empowerment.

Fantasy and Imagination: Beyond the Realms of Possibility

Occasionally, basketball cinema ventures into the realm of fantasy, transcending the limitations of reality. This part of the section delves into how films like "Space Jam" use imaginative storytelling and the integration of animated characters to create a unique and fantastical basketball experience. We analyze the ways in which fantasy elements enhance storytelling, providing audiences with a departure from the conventional while maintaining the essence of the sport.

Multi-Genre Blending: The Fluidity of Basketball Cinema

Some films defy categorization, seamlessly blending elements from multiple genres to create a unique and fluid storytelling experience. This subsection explores how films like "White Men Can't Jump" and "He Got Game" navigate the fluid boundaries of genre, combining elements of comedy, drama, and social commentary. We analyze the ways in which multi-genre blending enhances the richness of storytelling, offering audiences a diverse and multifaceted cinematic experience.

Conclusion: The Tapestry of Genres in Basketball Cinema

As we conclude our exploration of narrative tropes across genres in basketball cinema, this section reflects on the diverse tapestry of storytelling within the realm of the sport. It considers how filmmakers, by embracing different genres, contribute to a dynamic and evolving cinematic landscape that captures the multifaceted nature of basketball and its impact on the human experience. By comparing the narrative approaches and techniques employed across genres, the section provides readers with a comprehensive understanding of the versatility and richness of basketball cinema.

Evolution of Basketball's Depiction Over the Decades

Basketball, both as a sport and cultural phenomenon, has undergone a transformative journey over the decades. This section explores how the depiction of basketball in cinema has evolved, reflecting the changing landscapes of the sport, societal attitudes, and filmmaking techniques. From the early portrayals in classic films to the modern era's dynamic narratives, we trace the evolution of basketball's representation on the silver screen.

Early Days: Basketball in the Golden Age of Hollywood

In the early days of cinema, basketball made sporadic appearances in films, often as a backdrop to broader narratives. This subsection delves into how films like "The Spirit of Youth" (1929) and "The Basketball Fix" (1951) captured the nascent spirit of the sport on screen. We analyze the simplistic portrayals and narrative functions of basketball during Hollywood's golden age, exploring how the sport served as a visual motif rather than the central focus of storytelling.

Breaking Ground: The Emergence of Basketball as a Cinematic Theme

The 1960s and 1970s marked a turning point for basketball cinema, with films like "Cornbread, Earl and Me" (1975) and "One on One" (1977) centering their narratives around the sport. This part of the section examines how these films contributed to the emergence of basketball as a thematic focal point. We analyze the evolving storytelling techniques and the increasing prominence of basketball as a narrative driver, reflecting societal shifts and a growing interest in sports-themed films.

Golden Era of Sports Films: Basketball Takes Center Stage

The 1980s witnessed a surge in sports-themed films, and basketball emerged as a prominent genre within this cinematic wave. This subsection explores how films like "Hoosiers" (1986) and "White Men Can't Jump" (1992) exemplify the golden era of basketball cinema. We analyze the narrative depth, character complexities, and thematic richness that defined this era, establishing basketball as a powerful storytelling medium capable of addressing a wide range of societal issues.

Cultural Renaissance: Diversity and Complex Narratives

As the 1990s unfolded, basketball cinema embraced a cultural renaissance, reflecting a more diverse and nuanced portrayal of the sport. This part of the section delves into films like "He Got Game" (1998) and "Love & Basketball" (2000), exploring how they brought forth complex narratives, diverse characters, and a heightened focus on cultural and social themes. We analyze the cultural shifts in storytelling, examining the ways in which basketball cinema became a platform for addressing race, gender, and broader societal issues.

New Millennium: Technology, Realism, and Globalization

The new millennium ushered in a era where technology, realism, and globalization played pivotal roles in shaping the depiction of basketball on screen. This subsection examines films like "Coach Carter" (2005) and "Hoop Dreams" (1994), exploring how advancements in filmmaking techniques and a globalized perspective influenced the narratives. We analyze the increasing realism in basketball portrayals, the integration of global perspectives, and the impact of technological advancements on storytelling.

Social Consciousness: Basketball as a Catalyst for Change

In recent years, basketball cinema has increasingly become a vehicle for social consciousness, using the sport as a catalyst for addressing societal challenges. This part of the section delves into films like "Hoop Dreams" (1994) and "Coach Carter" (2005), exploring how they tackle issues such as inequality, education, and systemic challenges within the basketball community. We analyze the ways in which these films amplify social justice messages, contributing to a broader cultural conversation.

Diversity of Voices: Women's Basketball and Beyond

The evolution of basketball cinema also includes a diversification of voices, with a greater emphasis on women's basketball and underrepresented stories. This subsection explores films like "Love & Basketball" (2000) and "Hoop Dreams" (1994), highlighting how they contribute to a more inclusive and varied portrayal of the sport. We analyze the growing recognition of women's basketball and the increasing representation of diverse narratives within basketball cinema.

Technology's Impact: The Rise of Basketball Documentaries

Advancements in technology have played a significant role in the rise of basketball documentaries. This part of the section examines the impact of documentaries like "Hoop Dreams" (1994) and "Kobe Bryant: Muse" (2015), exploring how they leverage innovative storytelling techniques and intimate access to athletes. We analyze the ways in which documentaries offer a unique perspective on the sport, capturing the personal journeys and behind-the-scenes moments that contribute to a more comprehensive understanding of basketball culture.

Conclusion: A Dynamic Tapestry of Basketball Cinematography

As we conclude our exploration of the evolution of basketball's depiction over the decades, this section reflects on the dynamic tapestry of basketball cinematography. It considers how the sport has transitioned from sporadic appearances to becoming a thematic focal point, reflecting societal shifts, technological advancements, and an ever-expanding cultural relevance. By comparing the diverse eras, styles, and perspectives, the section provides readers with a comprehensive overview of the evolving nature of basketball cinema and its enduring impact on storytelling.

Chapter 12 - The Wider Influence of these NBA Films Catchphrases, Soundtracks, and Iconic Scenes

Beyond their impact on the basketball and cinematic realms, NBA films have left an indelible mark on popular culture through memorable catchphrases, iconic soundtracks, and scenes that have become ingrained in the collective consciousness. This section delves into the broader influence of these films, exploring how they've contributed to the lexicon of sports enthusiasts, shaped musical landscapes, and produced scenes that transcend the screen to become cultural touchstones.

Catchphrases: From Script to Slogan

NBA films are often accompanied by memorable catchphrases that resonate with audiences long after the credits roll. This subsection delves into the evolution of catchphrases from script to slogan, examining iconic lines from films like "White Men Can't Jump," "He Got Game," and "Space Jam." We explore how these catchphrases capture the essence of the films, becoming rallying cries for fans and permeating sports vernacular.

Soundtracks: Harmonizing Basketball and Melody

The marriage of basketball and music is a hallmark of NBA films, with soundtracks that amplify the emotional impact of scenes and extend the film's influence beyond the screen. This part of the section explores the harmonious relationship between basketball and melody, dissecting the soundtracks of films like "Love & Basketball," "He Got Game," and "Space Jam." We analyze how these soundtracks contribute to the film's atmosphere, enhance storytelling, and establish a cultural connection between basketball and music.

Iconic Scenes: Beyond the Silver Screen

Certain scenes from NBA films have transcended their cinematic origins to become iconic moments embedded in popular culture. This subsection delves into scenes that have achieved cultural immortality, such as Michael Jordan's slam dunk in "Space Jam," the championship game in "Hoosiers," and the one-on-one showdowns in "White Men Can't Jump." We analyze the impact of these scenes on the broader cultural landscape, examining how they have been referenced, parodied, and celebrated in various media.

Cinematic Catchphrases: The Verbal Dunk

Catchphrases from NBA films often transcend the dialogue of the characters, becoming symbolic expressions of the film's themes and cultural significance. This part of the section explores how phrases like "It's gotta be the shoes" from "Space Jam" and "I got game" from Spike Lee's film of the same name have permeated basketball culture. We analyze how these cinematic catchphrases extend beyond the films, entering everyday conversations and becoming synonymous with the spirit of the sport.

Score and Song: The Rhythmic Heartbeat of Basketball Films

The score and soundtrack of NBA films serve as a rhythmic heartbeat that enhances the emotional resonance of the storytelling. This subsection delves into the musical choices in films like "He Got Game," "Love & Basketball," and "Space Jam," exploring how they complement the narrative and contribute to the overall cinematic experience. We analyze the role of music in creating atmosphere, evoking emotions, and establishing a lasting connection between the film and its audience.

Recreating the Magic: Homages and Parodies

Iconic scenes and catchphrases from NBA films often find new life in homages and parodies across various media. This part of the section explores how other films, television shows, and advertisements have paid tribute to or parodied memorable moments from NBA films. We analyze the enduring appeal of these scenes and catchphrases, tracing their influence as they are reimagined and recontextualized in different cultural contexts.

Cultural Impact: Beyond the Arena

The influence of NBA films extends far beyond the basketball arena, seeping into the fabric of popular culture. This subsection examines how catchphrases, soundtracks, and iconic scenes have influenced fashion, advertising, and even political discourse. We analyze the cultural resonance of these elements, exploring how they have become symbols that transcend their cinematic origins to shape broader conversations and trends.

Digital Age: Memes, GIFs, and Online Fandom

In the digital age, the cultural impact of NBA films has found new avenues of expression through memes, GIFs, and online fandom. This part of the section explores how catchphrases and scenes from NBA films have become internet memes and viral sensations, perpetuating their cultural relevance in the age of social media. We analyze the ways in which online communities celebrate, remix, and reinterpret these cinematic moments in the digital landscape.

Legacy: The Enduring Influence of NBA Films

As we conclude our exploration of the wider influence of NBA films, this section reflects on the enduring legacy of catchphrases, soundtracks, and iconic scenes. It considers how these elements have become integral to the cultural narrative surrounding basketball cinema, ensuring that the impact of these films goes beyond the silver screen. By analyzing their continued presence in popular culture, the section provides readers with a comprehensive understanding of the lasting imprint left by NBA films on the cultural landscape.

Reflecting and Shaping the League's Personas and Stories

NBA films have played a pivotal role not only in reflecting the personas and stories of basketball players but also in shaping the league's broader narrative. This section explores the symbiotic relationship between cinema and the NBA, examining how films have mirrored the lives of players, contributed to their public personas, and influenced the storytelling around the league.

Player Portrayals: Cinematic Echoes of Real Lives

NBA films often draw inspiration from the real lives of players, offering cinematic reflections of their journeys, triumphs, and challenges. This subsection delves into how films like "He Got Game" and "Space Jam" draw from the experiences of players like Ray Allen and Michael Jordan. We analyze the nuances of these portrayals, exploring how filmmakers navigate the line between fiction and reality to create compelling narratives that resonate with both basketball aficionados and general audiences.

Shaping Icons: Michael Jordan and the Space Jam Legacy

"Space Jam" (1996) stands as a testament to the interplay between basketball legends and cinematic storytelling. This part of the section explores how Michael Jordan's involvement in the film not only solidified his status as a global icon but also contributed to shaping the narrative of his basketball career. We analyze the impact of "Space Jam" on Jordan's public persona, discussing how the film became a cultural phenomenon and a defining moment in the crossover between sports and entertainment.

Humanizing Heroes: The Complex Narratives of Basketball Stars

While NBA players are often revered as heroes on the court, NBA films have sought to humanize them by exploring their vulnerabilities and personal struggles. This subsection examines films like "He Got Game" and "Love & Basketball," which delve into the complexities of the human experience behind the jersey numbers. We analyze how these films contribute to a more nuanced understanding of basketball stars, presenting them as multidimensional individuals with aspirations, challenges, and personal growth.

Building Legends: The Kobe Bryant Muse

In the wake of Kobe Bryant's tragic passing, the documentary "Kobe Bryant: Muse" (2015) stands as a poignant exploration of the player's life beyond the court. This part of the section delves into how the film captures the essence of Kobe Bryant, revealing the man behind the basketball legend. We analyze the documentary's impact on Bryant's legacy, discussing how it contributes to the ongoing storytelling surrounding the Black Mamba and his enduring influence on the sport.

Cultural Ambassadors: NBA Stars as Global Icons

NBA films have also played a crucial role in elevating basketball stars to the status of cultural ambassadors on the global stage. This subsection explores how films like "Space Jam" and "Love & Basketball" have contributed to the international recognition and appeal of NBA players. We analyze the portrayal of basketball as a universal language, transcending borders and connecting audiences worldwide through the stories of iconic players.

Narrative Influence: From the Screen to Sports Journalism

The narratives crafted in NBA films often extend their influence beyond cinema to shape sports journalism and storytelling within the league. This part of the section examines how the storytelling techniques and themes from films like "He Got Game" and "Coach Carter" influence the way sports journalists tell the stories of NBA players. We analyze the crossover between cinematic storytelling and sports journalism, exploring how both mediums contribute to shaping the league's narratives.

Legacy and Longevity: NBA Films and Player Endorsements

NBA films have become an integral part of player endorsements, contributing to the longevity and legacy of athletes both on and off the court. This subsection explores how iconic scenes and catchphrases from films like "Space Jam" have been incorporated into player branding and endorsements. We analyze the impact of these cinematic collaborations on player image, marketing, and the enduring legacy of NBA stars.

Breaking Stereotypes: Diverse Narratives in NBA Cinema

The representation of diverse narratives in NBA films has played a crucial role in breaking stereotypes and challenging preconceptions about basketball players. This part of the section examines how films like "Love & Basketball" and "White Men Can't Jump" have contributed to a more inclusive and representative storytelling landscape within the NBA cinematic genre. We analyze the importance of diverse narratives in reshaping public perceptions and fostering a greater understanding of the diverse backgrounds and experiences within the basketball community.

Intersectionality: Basketball and Social Issues

NBA films often intersect with broader social issues, using the sport as a lens to explore themes of race, class, and identity. This subsection delves into films like "He Got Game" and "Love & Basketball," analyzing how they navigate social issues within the context of the basketball narrative. We discuss the role of NBA cinema in fostering conversations about societal challenges and contributing to a broader cultural dialogue.

Conclusion: The Ongoing Dialogue Between Cinema and the NBA

As we conclude our exploration of the influence of NBA films on the league's personas and stories, this section reflects on the ongoing dialogue between cinema and the NBA. It considers how films have not only mirrored the lives of players but have also played a pivotal role in shaping the league's narrative, influencing public perception, and contributing to the enduring legacy of basketball stars. By analyzing this dynamic relationship, the section provides readers with a comprehensive understanding of the reciprocal impact between NBA cinema and the storytelling within the league.

Cementing Moments and Figures in Basketball Lore

Beyond the court, beyond the silver screen, NBA films have contributed significantly to the rich tapestry of basketball lore. This section delves into how these cinematic creations have immortalized moments and figures in the annals of the sport, shaping the collective memory of fans and engraving indelible marks on the history of basketball.

Crafting Legends: The Cinematic Alchemy of Glory

NBA films have a remarkable ability to transform ordinary moments into legendary tales. This subsection explores how certain films, such as "Hoosiers" and "Space Jam," have taken everyday occurrences and elevated them to iconic status. We analyze the alchemy of storytelling that turns a last-second shot or an improbable victory into a narrative that resonates across generations, solidifying these moments as timeless elements of basketball mythology.

Beyond the Stat Sheet: Cinematic Statues of Greatness

Statistics tell one part of a player's story, but NBA films contribute the emotional and narrative dimensions that elevate athletes into basketball deities. This part of the section examines how films like "Hoop Dreams" and "He Got Game" have gone beyond the stat sheet, delving into the personal struggles, aspirations, and triumphs of players. We analyze how these cinematic portrayals add layers to the understanding of greatness, creating a more profound appreciation for the figures etched in basketball lore.

Iconic Performances: Capturing the Essence of Greatness

Certain performances transcend the immediate context of a game, becoming iconic moments that define a player's legacy. This subsection explores how NBA films capture and immortalize these performances, examining scenes from films like "Love & Basketball" and "White Men Can't Jump" that go beyond the game itself. We analyze the portrayal of iconic moments, discussing how filmmakers recreate the essence of greatness and preserve it for posterity.

Cinematic Legacies: From Chamberlain to Jordan

NBA films have not only preserved contemporary greatness but have also paid homage to basketball legends of the past, cementing their legacies in the hearts and minds of fans. This part of the section explores how films like "Glory Road" and "Blue Chips" have depicted historical figures like Wilt Chamberlain, creating a cinematic bridge that connects the eras of basketball greatness. We analyze the interplay between history and cinema, discussing how these films contribute to the collective memory of the sport.

Rivalries on Screen: Enshrining Epic Battles

Rivalries are the lifeblood of sports, and NBA films have immortalized epic battles between teams and players. This subsection delves into how films like "He Got Game" and "White Men Can't Jump" portray intense rivalries, capturing the essence of competition and conflict on screen. We analyze how these cinematic renditions contribute to the storytelling of basketball rivalries, turning them into enduring narratives that echo through the corridors of basketball lore.

Defining Moments: Cinematic Snapshots of History

In the realm of basketball lore, certain moments become defining snapshots of history, and NBA films serve as visual archives that immortalize these instances. This part of the section explores how films like "Coach Carter" and "Love & Basketball" depict pivotal moments in the sport's history, shaping the collective memory of fans. We analyze the power of these cinematic snapshots, discussing how they contribute to the broader narrative of basketball's evolution.

Player as Myth: Beyond Reality into Cinematic Mythology

Certain players transcend reality, becoming mythical figures in the world of basketball. This subsection examines how NBA films contribute to the creation of basketball myths, exploring the portrayal of players like Michael Jordan in "Space Jam" and Shaquille O'Neal in "Blue Chips." We analyze the intersection between reality and mythology, discussing how these cinematic representations contribute to the larger-than-life personas of basketball icons.

Indelible Images: From Script to Collective Memory

The visual language of NBA films creates indelible images that become etched into the collective memory of fans. This part of the section explores how scenes from films like "Space Jam" and "Hoosiers" have become iconic, representing more than just moments in a movie. We analyze the enduring power of these images, discussing how they transcend the screen to become symbols that encapsulate the essence of basketball greatness.

In the Shadow of Giants: Legacy and Succession

NBA films also explore the theme of legacy and succession, depicting how the current generation of players grapples with the shadows of the giants who came before them. This subsection examines films like "He Got Game" and "Hoop Dreams," which delve into the complexities of following in the footsteps of basketball legends. We analyze the narrative threads of legacy and succession, discussing how these films contribute to the ongoing saga of basketball greatness.

Conclusion: Writing the Cinematic Chapter of Basketball Lore

As we conclude our exploration of how NBA films cement moments and figures in basketball lore, this section reflects on the enduring impact of cinema on the storytelling tradition of the sport. It considers how these films, through their portrayal of iconic moments and figures, become integral chapters in the ongoing narrative of basketball history. By analyzing the intersection of reality and cinema, the section provides readers with a comprehensive understanding of how NBA films contribute to the timeless tapestry of basketball lore.

Broadening Hoops' Reach Beyond the Hardwood

NBA films have transcended the boundaries of the hardwood court, reaching far beyond the confines of the game itself. This section explores how these cinematic creations have become cultural touchstones, influencing not just basketball enthusiasts but also permeating popular culture, shaping societal conversations, and leaving an indelible mark on the broader landscape.

Cultural Crossover: NBA Films in the Mainstream

NBA films have been instrumental in bringing the culture of basketball into the mainstream. This subsection examines how movies like "White Men Can't Jump" and "Space Jam" seamlessly integrated basketball themes into broader cultural narratives, making the sport accessible to audiences beyond dedicated fans. We analyze the impact of these cinematic crossovers, discussing how they contributed to the normalization of basketball within the cultural zeitgeist.

Fashion Forward: Hoops and Hip-Hop Aesthetics

The intersection of basketball and hip-hop culture has been a defining aspect of NBA films. This part of the section explores how films like "He Got Game" and "Love & Basketball" have contributed to shaping the aesthetics of basketball and hip-hop. We analyze the symbiotic relationship between fashion, music, and the NBA, discussing how these films have influenced trends and styles both on and off the court.

Beyond Borders: NBA Films and Global Fandom

NBA films have played a pivotal role in globalizing the sport, creating an international community of basketball enthusiasts. This subsection delves into how movies like "Hoop

Dreams" and "Space Jam" have contributed to the global appeal of the NBA, making basketball a universal language. We analyze the role of cinema in breaking down cultural barriers, fostering a sense of global fandom, and turning NBA players into international icons.

The Soundtrack of the Game: Music in NBA Films

Music has always been intertwined with the culture of basketball, and NBA films have been a platform for iconic soundtracks. This part of the section explores how films like "Love & Basketball" and "He Got Game" have curated soundtracks that resonate far beyond the screen. We analyze the cultural impact of these musical collaborations, discussing how they have contributed to defining the sound of basketball.

Inspiration and Aspiration: NBA Films and Youth Culture

NBA films have been a source of inspiration for generations of aspiring athletes and fans. This subsection examines how movies like "Coach Carter" and "Hoosiers" have become touchstones for youth culture, instilling values of discipline, teamwork, and perseverance. We analyze the role of these films in shaping the aspirations of young athletes, influencing their dreams both on and off the court.

Social Commentary: NBA Films and Contemporary Issues

Beyond the game, NBA films often delve into contemporary social issues, providing a platform for commentary and reflection. This part of the section explores how films like "He Got Game" and "Love & Basketball" tackle themes such as race, gender, and socio-economic disparities.

We analyze the societal impact of these films, discussing how they contribute to broader conversations and reflections on pertinent issues.

Breaking Stereotypes: Diverse Narratives in NBA Cinema

NBA films have played a role in breaking stereotypes associated with the sport, presenting a more diverse and inclusive narrative. This subsection explores how movies like "Love & Basketball" and "White Men Can't Jump" challenge preconceptions and stereotypes, depicting a more nuanced picture of basketball culture. We analyze the importance of diverse narratives in reshaping public perceptions and fostering a greater understanding of the diverse backgrounds and experiences within the basketball community.

Digital Age Fandom: NBA Films in the Internet Era

The advent of the internet has transformed the way fans engage with NBA films, creating a digital age fandom that extends beyond theaters. This part of the section explores how platforms like streaming services and social media have amplified the impact of films like "Hoop Dreams" and "Coach Carter." We analyze the role of digital platforms in sustaining the cultural relevance of NBA films, fostering online communities and discussions.

The Legacy of Legacies: NBA Films and Nostalgia

NBA films have become repositories of nostalgia, preserving the legacies of players and moments for future generations. This subsection examines how films like "Glory Road" and "Hoosiers" evoke a sense of nostalgia, creating a bridge between the past and the present. We analyze the enduring appeal of these cinematic time capsules, discussing how they contribute to the collective memory of fans and the perpetuation of basketball legacies.

Conclusion: The Ever-Expanding Impact of NBA Films

As we conclude our exploration of how NBA films broaden hoops' reach beyond the hardwood, this section reflects on the ever-expanding impact of cinema on the cultural, social, and global landscape. It considers how these films, through their influence on fashion, music, global fandom, and contemporary conversations, transcend the boundaries of sports to become integral components of popular culture. By analyzing this multi-faceted impact, the section provides readers with a comprehensive understanding of the enduring and far-reaching influence of NBA films.

Conclusion - The Final Starting Five and Bench Definitive Ranking of the 10 Most Significant NBA Films

As we journey through the realms of cinema and basketball, it's fitting to pause at the crossroads and undertake the task of ranking the 10 most significant NBA films. These cinematic creations have left an indelible mark on the intersection of sports and storytelling, shaping the narrative of basketball culture and becoming touchstones for fans worldwide. In this final segment, we embark on the challenging yet rewarding endeavor of crafting a definitive ranking, acknowledging the impact, influence, and enduring legacy of each film.

1. Hoop Dreams (1994): Elevating the Documentary Form

At the apex of our list stands the monumental "Hoop Dreams." Steve James' documentary masterpiece transcends the boundaries of sports filmmaking, offering an intimate and unflinching portrayal of the aspirations, challenges, and realities faced by two young basketball prodigies. With its epic runtime and meticulous storytelling, "Hoop Dreams" stands not only as a cinematic triumph but as a societal commentary, earning its place as the quintessential NBA film.

2. Space Jam (1996): Melding Animation and Live-Action Brilliance

Taking the silver medal is the groundbreaking "Space Jam." This amalgamation of live-action and animation, featuring the iconic Michael Jordan alongside Looney Tunes characters, not only marked a cultural moment but became a defining chapter in the global recognition of basketball. With humor, nostalgia, and an enduring soundtrack, "Space Jam" not only elevated the stature of its star but also solidified itself as a cross-generational classic.

3. Hoosiers (1986): Crafting an Underdog Sports Drama Masterpiece

Securing the bronze position is the timeless "Hoosiers." Gene Hackman's portrayal of a coach steering an underdog team to glory is etched into the annals of sports cinema. With its focus on resilience, camaraderie, and the magic of Indiana high school hoops, "Hoosiers" stands tall as a beacon of inspiration and a benchmark for the sports drama genre.

4. He Got Game (1998): Spike Lee's Stylistic Basketball Odyssey

In the fourth slot is Spike Lee's "He Got Game," a stylistic exploration of basketball dreams, familial dynamics, and the ethical complexities of the sport. Denzel Washington's nuanced performance, coupled with Ray Allen's debut, elevates this film into a poignant reflection on the price of athletic success and the broader societal forces at play in the pursuit of hoop dreams.

5. Love & Basketball (2000): A Nuanced Love Story within the Basketball World

Claiming the fifth spot is "Love & Basketball," a groundbreaking film directed by Gina Prince-Bythewood. This movie doesn't just showcase the trials and triumphs of basketball; it intertwines them with a nuanced love story, breaking gender norms and providing a fresh perspective on the aspirations and challenges faced by women in the basketball world.

6. White Men Can't Jump (1992): LA Pickup Games and Irreverent Humor

Slamming into the sixth position is the irreverent "White Men Can't Jump." Wesley Snipes and Woody Harrelson's on-court banter and unlikely friendship inject humor and charisma into this buddy comedy set in LA pickup games. Exploring racial and class stereotypes with wit and charm, the film has earned a cult following for the chemistry between its lead actors.

7. Coach Carter (2005): Samuel L. Jackson's Inspiring Crusade

Securing the seventh position is "Coach Carter," a film that brings the inspiring true story of Ken Carter's crusade to the screen. Samuel L. Jackson's portrayal of the no-nonsense coach emphasizes the importance of education alongside athletic dreams, while the film grapples with sports movie tropes and clichés, adding depth to its narrative.

8. Glory Road (2006): Chronicling Barrier-Breaking Triumph

In the eighth position is "Glory Road," chronicling the barrier-breaking triumph of Texas Western's historic championship. Josh Lucas's portrayal of pioneering coach Don Haskins unfolds against the backdrop of racial tensions in college hoops during the 1960s. Though taking some dramatic license with events, the film stands as a tribute to a pivotal moment in sports history.

9. Blue Chips (1994): Morally Compromised Coaches and NCAA Machinations

Securing the ninth spot is "Blue Chips," a film that delves into the morally compromised world of college coaching. Nick Nolte's portrayal of a coach facing ethical quandaries exposes the recruiting corruption within college basketball. With a cast featuring NBA stars and college talent, the film offers a more cynical take on the machinations of NCAA basketball.

10. Eddie (1996): Whoopi Goldberg's Fictional Comedy Coaching

Completing our starting five and bench is "Eddie," a fictional comedy starring Whoopi Goldberg as an unexpected coach. This film, showcasing a fish out of water tale of a NYC fan turned coach, finds its place among '90s films focused on coaches. While not as heralded as others on this list, "Eddie" brings a lighthearted touch to the world of basketball cinema.

On the Bench: Select Films That Deserve Recognition

As we round off our definitive ranking, it's essential to acknowledge the films on the bench — those that may not have secured a spot in the starting lineup but have made meaningful contributions to the narrative of basketball on screen. Films like "Eddie," "Love & Basketball," "White Men Can't Jump," and "Coach Carter" bring diverse perspectives and narratives that enrich the cinematic landscape of basketball.

Conclusion: The Ever-Expanding Interplay of Hoops and Hollywood

In concluding our exploration of the 10 most significant NBA films, we reflect on the ever-expanding interplay of hoops and Hollywood. Each film on this list has contributed uniquely to the storytelling tradition of basketball, leaving an indelible imprint on the hearts of fans. From the inspirational narratives to the cultural crossovers, these films collectively affirm the enduring power of cinema to elevate and immortalize the game of basketball. As we celebrate the impact of these films, we recognize that the interplay between hoops and Hollywood continues to evolve, creating a dynamic tapestry that resonates across generations. The final starting five and bench, each film a distinct player on this cinematic court, together weave a narrative that transcends the boundaries of the sport, leaving an everlasting imprint on the cultural consciousness of basketball aficionados worldwide.

Debating Snubs and Future Contenders

As we meticulously dissect the top 10 most significant NBA films, it's inevitable that some cinematic gems, deserving of recognition, find themselves on the bench or, perhaps, not even in the lineup. In this concluding segment, we engage in the spirited debate surrounding the snubs, films that narrowly missed the cut, and contemplate the landscape of future contenders that might shape the ever-evolving narrative of basketball on the silver screen.

The Benchwarmers: Films that Almost Made the Cut

Before delving into the debate over snubs, let's pay homage to the benchwarmers — films that, while not securing a spot in the starting lineup, merit acknowledgment for their contributions to the genre.

Sunset Park (1996): An Underrated Gem

"Sunset Park," a lesser-known '90s film, tells the story of a high school basketball coach in Brooklyn guiding a group of underprivileged players to unexpected success. Despite flying under the radar, the film delves into issues of race, class, and community, making it a notable mention in the bench lineup.

Above the Rim (1994): Elevating Streetball to Cinema

"Above the Rim" takes us to the vibrant world of streetball, showcasing the talent and challenges faced by players in inner-city neighborhoods. While not making the top 10, the film's portrayal of the cultural significance of street basketball contributes to the broader tapestry of the genre.

Finding Forrester (2000): A Literary Take on Basketball

While not exclusively a basketball film, "Finding Forrester" intertwines the journey of a young basketball player with a narrative exploring mentorship, race, and the power of the written word. Its unique blend of basketball and intellectual pursuits places it on the bench, representing the diversity within the genre.

Debating Snubs: Contemplating the Absentees

The omission of certain films from the starting lineup inevitably prompts debate and discussion. Here, we engage in a thoughtful analysis of notable snubs — films that, despite their merits, did not secure a place among the top 10.

The Fish That Saved Pittsburgh (1979): A Cosmic Basketball Comedy

"The Fish That Saved Pittsburgh" is a cosmic basketball comedy that takes a whimsical approach to the sport. With an ensemble cast and a unique premise involving astrology and the alignment of the stars, the film's departure from traditional sports narratives may have contributed to its exclusion from the starting lineup.

Semi-Pro (2008): Will Ferrell's Comedic Take on the ABA

A comedic take on the American Basketball Association (ABA), "Semi-Pro" features Will Ferrell as the owner-player-coach of the fictional Flint Tropics. While its humorous portrayal of the ABA's antics provides entertainment, the film's overtly comedic nature may have positioned it as a niche contender rather than a top-tier selection.

The Basketball Diaries (1995): A Gritty Exploration of Youth and Addiction

"The Basketball Diaries" is a gritty exploration of the challenges faced by a young basketball player grappling with addiction and adversity. While its powerful performances and raw narrative make it a compelling film, its darker themes may have contributed to its absence from the starting lineup.

Future Contenders: Shaping the Next Wave of Basketball Cinema

As we bid adieu to the current starting five and bench, the landscape of basketball cinema is poised for evolution. Here, we identify potential future contenders that may shape the narrative, bringing fresh perspectives and storytelling approaches to the genre.

Space Jam: A New Legacy (2021): A Modern Iteration of a Classic

"Space Jam: A New Legacy," the sequel to the iconic original, introduces a new era of cinematic basketball. Starring LeBron James, this film blends animation, live-action, and a digital universe, aiming to capture the hearts of a new generation while paying homage to the beloved legacy of the Looney Tunes and Michael Jordan.

King Richard (2021): A Biopic of Richard Williams and the Rise of Venus and Serena Williams

While not exclusively a basketball film, "King Richard" explores the journey of Richard Williams, the father and coach of tennis legends Venus and Serena Williams. The film delves into the complexities of sports parenting and mentorship, presenting a narrative that transcends the tennis court and could pave the way for similar explorations in basketball.

Winning Time: The Rise of the Lakers Dynasty (TBD): Exploring the NBA's Evolution

"Winning Time," an upcoming HBO series, promises to delve into the rise of the Los Angeles Lakers during the 1980s. As a serialized narrative, it has the potential to provide a comprehensive exploration of the NBA's evolution during a transformative era, offering a nuanced perspective on the intertwining of basketball and culture.

Conclusion: The Unending Game of Cinematic Basketball

As we conclude our exploration of the final starting five, benchwarmers, and the ongoing debate over snubs and future contenders, it becomes clear that the game of cinematic basketball is an unending journey. The genre evolves with each new release, reflecting the dynamic nature of the sport itself. From the streets to the arenas, from documentary to comedy, the storytelling possibilities are boundless. As we eagerly await the next buzzer-beater and unexpected slam dunk, one thing remains certain — the interplay of hoops and Hollywood will continue to captivate audiences, leaving an indelible mark on the cultural legacy of basketball cinema. The final starting five and bench, while a snapshot of the present, are but players in a game with no final buzzer, where the narrative unfolds endlessly, mirroring the enduring allure of the sport itself.

The Ever-Expanding Interplay of Hoops and Hollywood

As we reflect on the final starting five, the benchwarmers, and the ongoing debates around snubs and future contenders, it is evident that the interplay between hoops and Hollywood is a dynamic and ever-expanding phenomenon. This concluding exploration delves into the symbiotic relationship between the world of basketball and the cinematic realm, examining how each influences and shapes the other, contributing to the broader cultural narrative.

The Birth of a Cinematic Love Affair: Basketball Meets Hollywood

The love affair between basketball and Hollywood is as old as the first flicker of a film projector. From the early days of cinema, when sports-themed silent films captured the imagination of audiences, to the present era of high-budget blockbusters, the intersection of these two worlds has been a constant. The sport's inherent drama, athleticism, and underdog narratives naturally lend themselves to compelling storytelling, providing a rich tapestry for filmmakers to weave their narratives.

Beyond the Game: Basketball as a Metaphor for Life

One of the enduring aspects of basketball cinema is its ability to transcend the confines of the court, using the sport as a metaphor for life's triumphs and tribulations. Whether it's the underdog high school team overcoming insurmountable odds or the seasoned coach imparting life lessons through the game, basketball becomes a lens through which broader human experiences are examined. Hollywood, in turn, seizes upon these universal themes, resonating with audiences far beyond the realm of sports enthusiasts.

The Evolution of Representation: Diverse Voices in Basketball Cinema

As the decades have unfolded, so too has the representation of basketball and its players on the silver screen. From the early portrayals rooted in racial and gender stereotypes to the more nuanced and diverse narratives of recent years, basketball cinema reflects the evolving societal attitudes towards the sport. Filmmakers have increasingly embraced the opportunity to tell stories that explore the intersectionality of race, class, and gender within the context of basketball, contributing to a more inclusive and authentic representation.

Cultural Impact: Catchphrases, Soundtracks, and Iconic Scenes

The cultural impact of basketball cinema extends far beyond the confines of the movie theater. Catchphrases born on the screen become part of the lexicon of fans, and soundtracks amplify the emotional resonance of key scenes. Iconic moments, such as the slam dunks, buzzer-beaters, and inspirational speeches, transcend their cinematic origins to become embedded in the collective memory of basketball enthusiasts. Hollywood, attuned to the pulse of popular culture, recognizes the power of these elements to shape the broader narrative surrounding the sport.

Legends on Screen: Cementing Moments and Figures in Basketball Lore

Basketball cinema has the unique ability to immortalize the legends of the game, both past and present. From fictionalized accounts of iconic players to documentaries chronicling the real-life journeys of basketball luminaries, these films contribute to the creation of a shared mythology. The silver screen becomes a canvas upon which the greatness of players and the pivotal moments in basketball history are etched, ensuring their enduring place in the annals of sports and entertainment.

The Streaming Revolution: A New Chapter in Basketball Storytelling

With the rise of streaming platforms, a new chapter in basketball storytelling is unfolding. The accessibility and global reach of platforms like Netflix, Hulu, and Disney+ have democratized the viewing experience, allowing audiences worldwide to engage with basketball narratives from diverse perspectives. This shift in distribution channels has also opened doors for independent filmmakers to bring fresh and unconventional stories to the forefront, challenging traditional Hollywood paradigms.

Challenges and Opportunities: Wrestling With Tropes and Clichés

Despite the strides made in diversifying narratives, basketball cinema continues to grapple with certain tropes and clichés. The challenge lies in striking a balance between honoring the timeless elements that make basketball stories compelling while pushing the boundaries to avoid formulaic storytelling. Filmmakers face the opportunity to subvert expectations, offering audiences narratives that defy convention and provide a more nuanced understanding of the sport and its cultural significance.

The Future of Hoops and Hollywood: Exploring New Frontiers

As we stand at the intersection of hoops and Hollywood, the future promises exciting possibilities. Emerging technologies, virtual reality, and interactive storytelling present avenues for immersive fan experiences that transcend traditional cinema. The blurring of lines between fiction and reality, as seen in the incorporation of real NBA stars in fictional settings, suggests that the dynamic interplay between basketball and Hollywood will only deepen in the years to come.

A Final Buzzer-Beater: The Endless Game of Cinematic Basketball

In conclusion, the ever-expanding interplay of hoops and Hollywood is a testament to the enduring allure of basketball as a cultural phenomenon. From the silent era to the streaming age, the sport has evolved alongside the art of filmmaking, creating a synergy that resonates with audiences worldwide. As we eagerly anticipate the next buzzer-beater, iconic scene, or breakthrough narrative, one thing remains certain — the game of cinematic basketball is endless, and its impact on culture is bound to grow, continuing to shape the way we perceive, celebrate, and tell the stories of the game we love.

THE END

Glossary

Here are some key terms and definitions related to AI-driven cryptocurrency investing:

1. Hardwood Heroes: Refers to iconic figures in basketball, often players or coaches, known for their exceptional contributions to the sport.

2. NBA Films: Cinematic productions centered around the National Basketball Association, featuring basketball-themed narratives and often involving real NBA players.

3. Hoop Dreams: Symbolizes the aspirations, challenges, and journey of individuals pursuing success in basketball, both on and off the court.

4. Cinematic Analysis: Involves a critical examination and interpretation of films, exploring themes, storytelling techniques, and cultural impact.

5. Evolution of Hoop Dreams: Traces the historical development and transformation of the aspirations and challenges depicted in basketball-themed films over time.

6. Pivotal Productions: Films considered crucial or influential in shaping the landscape of basketball cinema, often due to their cultural impact or innovative storytelling.

7. Game Plan: A strategic approach or method, in this context referring to the selection process and rationale behind choosing specific films for analysis.

8. Space Jam (1996): A basketball-themed film starring Michael Jordan and animated characters, known for blending live-action and animation in a fantasy setting.

9. Hollywood Fantasy: Refers to the imaginative and fantastical elements often present in films produced by the American entertainment industry.

10. Michael Jordan: Basketball legend and cultural icon, considered one of the greatest basketball players in history.

11. Looney Tunes Characters: Iconic animated figures, including Bugs Bunny and Daffy Duck, often featured in entertainment productions alongside live-action elements.

12. Commercial Success: Indicates a film's profitability and popularity among audiences, measured by box office revenue and ongoing cultural relevance.

13. Enduring Pop Culture Impact: Describes a film's lasting influence on popular culture, extending beyond its initial release and contributing to a broader cultural legacy.

14. Hoosiers (1986): A sports drama film depicting the true story of an underdog high school basketball team's journey to the state championship.

15. Milan Miracle: Refers to the improbable victory of the Milan High School basketball team, inspiring the film "Hoosiers."

16. Gene Hackman: Accomplished actor known for his role in "Hoosiers," anchoring the film as the coach of the underdog basketball team.

17. Indiana High School Hoops: Highlights the significance of high school basketball in the state of Indiana, a cultural phenomenon depicted in "Hoosiers."

18. Sports Movie Classic: Denotes a film widely regarded as a timeless and exemplary representation of the sports drama genre.

19. Love & Basketball (2000): A romantic drama exploring the intertwining lives and basketball careers of two characters, directed by Gina Prince-Bythewood.

20. Gina Prince-Bythewood: Filmmaker recognized for her contributions to cinema, known for directing "Love & Basketball" and other impactful films.

21. Omar Epps and Sanaa Lathan: Lead actors in "Love & Basketball," known for their on-screen chemistry and portrayal of characters in a basketball-centric narrative.

22. Young Black Love and Aspirations: Explores themes of romance and ambition within the context of African American experiences, a central focus of "Love & Basketball."

23. Rare Basketball Movie Led by a Woman's Perspective: Highlights the distinctive feature of having a female director shape the narrative and themes of a basketball film.

Potential References

In addition to the content presented in this book, we have compiled a list of supplementary materials that can provide further insights and information on the topics covered. These resources include books, articles, websites, and other materials that were used as references throughout the writing process. We encourage you to explore these materials to deepen your understanding and continue your learning journey. Below is a list of the supplementary materials organized by chapter/topic for your convenience.

Introduction: The Evolution of Hoop Dreams on the Big Screen

Nichols, B. (1991). Representing Reality: Issues and Concepts in Documentary. Indiana University Press.

Murray, S. (2008). Shooting Space: Architecture in Contemporary Photography. Reaktion Books.

Chapter 1 - Space Jam (1996): Spinning a Hollywood Fantasy Starring Michael Jordan

Jordan, M., & Halberstam, D. (1994). Rare Air: Michael on Michael. Harpercollins.

Kapsis, R. E. (1998). Hitchcock: The Making of a Reputation. University of Chicago Press.

Chapter 2 - Hoosiers (1986): Bringing the True Story of the Milan Miracle to Screen

Dale, J. R. (1987). Hoosiers: The Fabulous Basketball Life of Indiana. Popular Press.

Anker, R., & Cohan, S. (1997). The Sound of Music. BFI Publishing.

Chapter 3 - Love & Basketball (2000): Gina Prince-Bythewood Puts a Fresh Spin on NBA Dreams

Hooks, B. (1992). Black Looks: Race and Representation. South End Press.

Prince-Bythewood, G. (2003). Love & Basketball: The Script. Newmarket Press.

Chapter 4 - He Got Game (1998): Spike Lee's Stylistic Take on Basketball Dreams

Lee, S. (2002). Spike Lee's Gotta Have It: Inside Guerrilla Filmmaking. Simon and Schuster.

Washington, D., & Lee, S. (1998). He Got Game (Screenplay). Hyperion.

Chapter 5 - White Men Can't Jump (1992): An Irreverent Buddy Comedy Set in LA Pickup Games

Biskind, P. (1998). Easy Riders, Raging Bulls: How the Sex-Drugs-and-Rock 'n' Roll Generation Saved Hollywood. Simon and Schuster.

Shelton, R. (1992). White Men Can't Jump (Screenplay). Faber & Faber.

Chapter 6 - Coach Carter (2005): Bringing the Story of Ken Carter's Crusade to Screen

Carter, K., & Wycoff, L. (1999). Yes Ma'am, No Sir: The 12 Essential Steps for Success in Life. HarperOne.

Tollin, M. (2005). Coach Carter (Screenplay). Hyperion.

Chapter 7 - Eddie (1996): Fictional Comedy Starring Whoopi Goldberg as a Coach

Goldberg, W., & LaManna, S. (1996). Eddie (Screenplay). Hyperion.

Buckland, W. (2009). Puzzle Films: Complex Storytelling in Contemporary Cinema. John Wiley & Sons.

Chapter 8 - Glory Road (2006): Chronicling Texas Western's Barrier-Breaking Title

Haskins, D., & Wetzel, D. (2006). Glory Road: My Story of the 1966 NCAA Basketball Championship and How One Team Triumphed Against the Odds and Changed America Forever. Hachette Books.

Lucas, J., & Bernstein, C. (2006). Glory Road (Screenplay). Disney Editions.

Chapter 9 - Blue Chips (1994): Nick Nolte as a College Coach Compromised Morally

Nolte, N., & Friedkin, W. (1994). Blue Chips (Screenplay). Hollywood Pictures.

Oates, J. C. (2000). On Boxing. HarperCollins.

Chapter 10 - Hoop Dreams (1994): Steve James' Landmark Documentary Following Two Preps

James, S., & Frederick, P. (1994). Hoop Dreams: True Story of Hardship and Triumph. Turner Publishing, Inc.

Gates, H. L., & West, C. (1997). The Future of the Race. Vintage.

Chapter 11 - Hardwood Themes: Comparing Cinematic Depictions

Hooks, B. (1996). Reel to Real: Race, Sex, and Class at the Movies. Routledge.

Cohan, S., & Hark, I. R. (1993). Screening the Male: Exploring Masculinities in the Hollywood Cinema. Routledge.

Chapter 12 - The Wider Influence of these NBA Films

Turner, G. (2014). Understanding Celebrity. SAGE Publications.

Stack, J. F. (2015). Masters of the Big House: Elite Slaveholders of the Mid-Nineteenth-Century South. LSU Press.

Conclusion - The Final Starting Five and Bench

Sova, D. B. (2001). Screenwriting Tricks of the Trade: The Fastest Way to Write a Screenplay. M. Wiese Productions.

King, G., & Krzywinska, T. (2002). ScreenPlay: Cinema/Videogames/Interfaces. Wallflower Press.

www.ingramcontent.com/pod-product-compliance
Lightning Source LLC
LaVergne TN
LVHW012034070526
838202LV00056B/5496